David Clarke
Ingrid Preedy

Besser in Englisch

5. Klasse

Cornelsen
Power Learning

Diese Lernhilfe gibt es auch mit CD-ROM:
Cornelsen Power Learning Englisch 5. Klasse
(ISBN 3-589-21508-9)

Cornelsen online http://www.cornelsen.de

Gedruckt auf chlorfrei gebleichtem Papier
ohne Dioxinbelastung der Gewässer.

Bibliografische Information
Die Deutsche Bibliothek verzeichnet diese Publikation in der Deutschen Nationalbibliografie; detaillierte bibliografische Daten sind im Internet über **http://dnb.ddb.de** abrufbar.

Dieses Werk berücksichtigt die Regeln der reformierten Rechtschreibung und Zeichensetzung.

5.	4.	3.	2.	1.	Die letzten Ziffern bezeichnen
07	06	05	04	03	Zahl und Jahr der Auflage.

Redaktion: Sigrid Janssen, Hannover; Helga Holtkamp, Berlin
Redaktionelle Mitarbeit: Andrew Dowdall, Berlin
Gesamtgestaltung: Dagmar & Torsten Lemme, Berlin
Umschlagentwurf: Bauer + Möhring, Berlin
Illustrationen: Katharina Siegers, Berlin; Constanze Schargan, Berlin
Repro: City Repro, Berlin
Druck und Bindung: Tesinska Tiskarna, Cesky Tesin
Printed in the Czech Republic
ISBN 3-589-21816-9
Bestellnummer 218169

Inhalt

Wenn du wissen willst, was du schon kannst oder was du besonders üben musst, mach zuerst die *Fast lane* oder *Super fast lane*. Hast du die nötige Punktzahl erreicht, kannst du das Kapitel überspringen. In der *Fast lane* stehen Aufgaben zu einem Kapitel, in der *Super fast lane* Aufgaben zu mehreren Kapiteln eines Themenbereichs.

Vorwort

Liebe Schülerin, lieber Schüler!
Du hast hier ein Buch zum Lernen, Wiederholen und Üben in der Hand.
Die Themen sind in kleinen, verständlichen Schritten aufbereitet.
An vielen Stellen kannst du selbst in das Buch hineinschreiben.
Kontrolliere deine Ergebnisse mit dem Lösungsheft.

Mit diesem Buch kannst du auf *zweierlei Weise* arbeiten:

1. **Möglichkeit:**
   Du fühlst dich insgesamt in Englisch unsicher. Dann arbeite das Buch von vorne bis hinten durch. Nimm dir nicht zu viel auf einmal vor. Bearbeite lieber kleinere Abschnitte, aber dafür regelmäßig, vielleicht sogar täglich.
2. **Möglichkeit:**
   Du kennst deine Lücken. Du weißt, bei welchen Aufgabenstellungen du noch unsicher bist. Dann sieh im Inhaltsverzeichnis nach, picke einzelne Abschnitte heraus, und arbeite sie durch.

Und noch einige praktische Tipps zum Lernen mit diesem Buch:

- Verwende zum Eintragen ins Buch einen Bleistift. Fehler kannst du dann leichter ausbessern.
- Bist du dir beim Lösen der Übungsaufgaben nicht ganz sicher, sieh dir die Beispiele noch einmal genau an.
- Vergleiche deine Ergebnisse mit dem Lösungsheft. Überprüfe bei Fehlern immer genau, was du falsch gemacht hast.
- Bearbeite die Übungsaufgaben nach einigen Tagen noch einmal. So kannst du zusätzliche Sicherheit gewinnen.

Die *Symbole* am Seitenrand bedeuten:

Wichtige Regel: Präge sie dir genau ein.

Vokabelübung: Erweitere und festige deinen Wortschatz.

Übungsaufgabe: Löse sie im Buch oder Heft.

Beispiel: Es zeigt dir, wie es richtig ist.

Überprüfe, ob du den Stoff schon beherrschst.

Dieses Buch gehört:
Name:
Straße:
Ort:

Wir stellen uns vor!

Du triffst uns in diesem Buch ...

1 Das Nomen

A Die regelmäßige Form des Plurals

B Unregelmäßige Formen des Plurals

C Der *'s*- und der *of*-Genitiv

A Die regelmäßige Form des Plurals

❶ There are 28 **boys** and **girls** in Miss Jones' class. They go to school five **days** a week, and have eight **lessons** a day.
❷ Adam Clarke can drink three **glasses** of coke, he can eat eight **sandwiches** and two **boxes** of biscuits.
❸ There are special tickets for **families** with small **babies** on **buses** and **trains**.
❹ Kirsty, can you please get the **knives** and **forks**?

▶ Bei den meisten Nomen (Hauptwörtern) bilden wir den Plural durch das einfache Anhängen von *-s* ❶.

▶ Wenn der Singular in einem Zischlaut *(-s, -sh, -ch, -x oder -z)* endet, wird *-es* angehängt ❷.

▷ Beachte:

famil**y** – famil**ies**	kni**fe** – kni**ves**	tomato – tomat**oes**
bab**y** – bab**ies**	wi**fe** – wi**ves**	potat**o** – potat**oes**

Exercise 1

Bilde den Plural der unten aufgeführten Nomen.

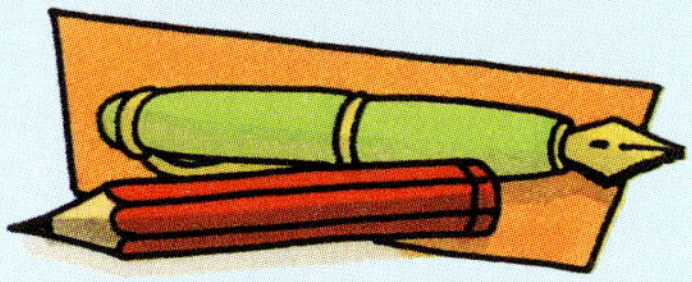

1 At school

chair	– ____________	class	– ____________
desk	– ____________	felt tip	– ____________
girl	– ____________	lesson	– ____________
pen	– ____________	pencil	– ____________
shelf	– ____________	table	– ____________

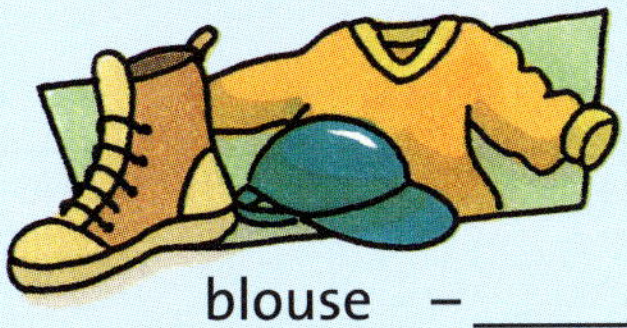

2 Clothes

blouse	– ____________	coat	– ____________
dress	– ____________	jacket	– ____________
pullover	– ____________	shoe	– ____________

3 Food and drink

apple	– ____________	biscuit	– ____________
cake	– ____________	cheese	– ____________
drink	– ____________	orange	– ____________
potato	– ____________	sandwich	– ____________
sausage	– ____________	tomato	– ____________

4 Transport

bicycle	– ____________	bus	– ____________
car	– ____________	lorry	– ____________
plane	– ____________	ship	– ____________
taxi	– ____________	train	– ____________
van	– ____________	wheel	– ____________

B Unregelmäßige Formen des Plurals

❶ – Many **children** clean their **teeth** after every meal.
– And what about **men** and **women**?
❷ Look at your **feet**, Tom. They're black! Go and wash them.

▷ Einige Nomen haben einen unregelmäßigen Plural, zum Beispiel:

child – **children**
man – **men**
woman – **women** ['wɪmɪn]
tooth – **teeth**
foot – **feet**

Exercise 2

Wie viele der Gegenstände, Personen usw. auf dem Bild kannst du dir merken, ohne nochmals nachzusehen?
Decke das Bild ab und schreibe auf, was du gesehen hast.

Super fast lane

Setze die Nomen in Klammern in der richtigen Form in den Text ein.
Pass dabei gut auf, weil einige in der Einzahl bleiben müssen.

✔ = richtig ✘ = falsch

The ________________ (child) in Miss Jones' ________________ (class) are very excited *(aufgeregt)*. They are planning a class ________________ (party), and they think that ________________ (party) are great. Miss Jones is talking to the ________________ (boy) and ________________ (girl) about everything they must do. "What about ________________ (knife) and ________________ (fork)?" she says. "And who can bring some ________________ (cup) and ________________ (glass)?" "I can," says Amy. Miss Jones writes down Amy's ________________ (name) on one of her ________________ (list). "Now," she says, "let's talk about the ________________ (food). What would you like to have?" "Oh," says Adam, "lots of lovely ________________ (biscuit), chocolate ________________ (cake) and ________________ (sweet), of course, Miss." "Don't be a silly ________________ (boy), Adam," says Miss Jones. "Sweet ________________ (thing) are very bad for your ________________ (tooth)."

Weniger als 13 Punkte? Wenn ja, arbeite bitte Kapitel 1 A und 1 B nochmals durch!

max. 19

C Der *'s*- und der *of*-Genitiv

1. Amy Cobb is **Tom's sister** and **Bob's girlfriend**.
2. My **sister's room** is always tidy.
3. The **boys' uniform** is nice and the **girls' uniform** is nice, too.
4. The new shop has **men's, women's** and **children's clothes**.
5. **The name of the street** is Oak Lane, and Adam lives at **the end of the street**.

- Bei Personen (und auch Haustieren) verwenden wir den *'s*-Genitiv ❶ – ❹.
- Wenn das Nomen im Singular steht, hängen wir einfach *'s* an ❷.
- Wenn der Plural oder Singular auf *-s* endet, hängen wir nur *'* an ❸.
- Wenn der Plural nicht auf *-s* endet, verwenden wir ebenfalls *'s* ❹.
- Bei Sachen verwenden wir die *of*-Form des Genitivs ❺.

Exercise 3

Schreibe auf, wem bzw. zu was die abgebildeten Sachen gehören.

1 Amy's dog ______ 5 ______

2 ______ 6 ______

3 ______ 7 ______

4 ______ 8 ______

Fast lane

Übersetze die unterstrichenen Teile der Sätze ins Englische.

✔ = richtig ✘ = falsch

1 Wir spielen oft im Garten meiner Eltern.

______

2 Amys Hund, Spooky, und Mrs Cobbs Vogel, Tweets, mögen gern Schokolade.

______

______

3 Mr Parker streicht das Fenster von Bobs Zimmer.

______

4 Adams Haus ist am Ende der Straße.

______

______

5 Toms Mathebuch ist dreckig und sechs Seiten des Buches fehlen.

______

______

6 Die Farbe seiner Augen ist grün.

______

7 Die Ärmel *(sleeves)* von Kirstys Kleid sind zu kurz.

______

Weniger als 7 Punkte? Wenn ja, arbeite bitte Kapitel 1 C nochmals durch!

max. 10

Hidden countries

Suche waagerecht (→), senkrecht (↓) und diagonal (↘) nach den Ländern, die sich hier verbergen. Kreise sie ein und schreibe sie auf.

A	D	R	P	L	E	R	Z	T	I	U	S
P	O	R	T	U	G	A	L	S	S	E	C
F	A	L	F	A	T	L	A	P	L	I	O
A	U	S	T	R	A	L	I	A	I	A	T
M	E	N	G	E	A	J	N	I	R	B	L
E	E	N	G	L	A	N	D	N	E	U	A
R	Q	H	L	E	S	I	C	D	L	I	N
I	E	S	A	N	R	K	L	E	A	N	D
C	I	E	L	J	D	M	N	C	N	J	L
A	U	S	T	R	I	A	A	A	D	S	E
R	E	G	T	O	P	B	A	N	A	L	A
E	U	W	E	A	D	E	F	H	Y	K	T

1 ______________________

2 ______________________

3 ______________________

4 ______________________

5 ______________________

6 ______________________

7 ______________________

8 ______________________

9 ______________________

10 ______________________

Holiday

Die Buchstaben ergeben richtig geordnet ein Wort, mit dem du den zugehörigen Satz vervollständigen sollst.

1 A H L I D O Y

In summer, many people go on _ _ _ _ _ _ _ .

2 N T I R A

In Germany, it is easy to travel by bus or _ _ _ _ _ .

3 P O C A T R S D S

When you are on holiday, you often send _ _ _ _ _ _ _ _ _ to your friends at home.

4 T S B R A E K A F

In England, it's cheap to stay in a Bed and _ _ _ _ _ _ _ _ _ .

5 P A L E N

When you travel to America, you need to go by _ _ _ _ _ .

6 C P S T E A M I

If you take a tent on holiday, you usually stay on a _ _ _ _ _ _ _ _ .

7 S U N G E L S A S S

When the sun is shining brightly, it's good to wear _ _ _ _ _ _ _ _ _ _.

8 H E A B C

It's nice to go to the _ _ _ _ _ when the weather is hot.

9 O J Y E U N R

It's a long _ _ _ _ _ _ _ from Edinburgh to London.

10 O S M T A N I U N

Every winter we go skiing in the _ _ _ _ _ _ _ _ _ .

2 Die Pronomen

A Die Personalpronomen

B Die *possessive adjectives*

C Die Demonstrativpronomen

A Die Personalpronomen

❶ Tom is Amy's brother. **He** is Bob's friend.
❷ Amy is Bob's girlfriend. **She** often watches the boys when **they** play football. **She** enjoys **it** very much.
❸ – Can **you** tell **me** where Tom is?
– Yes. **I** can see **him** in the garden.
❹ – Does Mr Carter give **you** a lot of homework?
– **He** usually gives **us** so much that I haven't got time to go out.

▶ Wir benutzen Pronomen, um eine eintönige Wiederholung von Namen zu vermeiden.

▷ Hier ist eine Übersicht der Personalpronomen mit den deutschen Bedeutungen:

Subjektform		**Objektform**			
			Wem?		**Wen?**
I	*ich*	me	*mir*	me	*mich*
you	*du/Sie*	you	*dir/Ihnen*	you	*dich/Sie*
he	*er*	him	*ihm*	him	*ihn*
she	*sie*	her	*ihr*	her	*sie*
it	*es*	it	*ihm/ihr*	it	*es/ihn/sie*
we	*wir*	us	*uns*	us	*uns*
you	*ihr/Sie*	you	*euch/Ihnen*	you	*euch/Sie*
they	*sie*	them	*ihnen*	them	*sie*

Exercise 1

Ersetze alle Namen mit Pronomen in der Subjektform.
Trage die Pronomen rechts ein.

1 Tom goes to school by bike. *he*

2 Amy has cornflakes for breakfast. ______

3 Kirsty has got some new shoes. ______

4 The Rolls-Royce is standing in front of the house. ______

5 Bob, Tom and Adam all live in Oak Lane. ______

6 Miss Jones teaches in Kingston. ______

7 Fiats and Ferraris are cars from Italy. ______

Exercise 2

Ersetze alle Namen mit Pronomen in der Objektform.
Trage die Pronomen rechts ein.

1 We all like Miss Jones. *her*

2 The dog is running after Adam. ______

3 My mother is visiting Mr and Mrs Parker. ______

4 The boys are meeting Kirsty and Amy. ______

5 The policeman is stopping the BMW in King Street. ______

6 Bob is giving Amy a box of chocolates. ______

7 Mr Carter teaches the boys and girls maths. ______

Fast lane

Trage die fehlenden Pronomen sowohl in der Subjektform als auch in der Objektform ein.

✔ = richtig ✘ = falsch

My mother is meeting the girls. ______ are in the shop.

My mother is talking to ______ . ______ are telling

______ that ______ are looking for a present for Adam.

But _____ don't know what to buy _____ . My mother says to _____ that she thinks it's a good idea to get _____ a CD, but the girls say _____ don't want to buy a CD. _____ think _____ is too expensive. Amy says _____ thinks that a cap is a good idea but Kirsty thinks _____ is a silly idea. _____ says Adam already has a cap, and _____ doesn't like _____ . Suddenly Adam comes into the shop. " _____ know that _____ are talking about _____ ", _____ says.
" _____ don't know what to buy _____ for my birthday. Well, _____ want lots of sweets for my birthday. _____ know how much _____ love _____ ."

Weniger als 18 Punkte? Wenn ja, arbeite bitte Kapitel 2 A nochmals durch!

max. 27

B Die *possessive adjectives*

❶ Adam is eating **his** dinner.
❷ Amy is doing **her** homework.
❸ We sometimes do **our** maths homework on the bus.
❹ Bob and Tom do **their** homework together.
❺ Don't forget to clean **your** teeth and comb **your** hair, Tom.

▶ Die *possessive adjectives* zeigen an, wem etwas gehört, und stehen direkt vor dem Nomen ❶ – ❹.

▶ Das *possessive adjective* wird im Englischen auch für Körperteile verwendet ❺.

▷ Hier ist eine Übersicht der *possessive adjectives*:

I	**my**	we	**our**
you	**your**	you	**your**
he	**his**	they	**their**
she	**her**		
it	**its**		

Exercise 3

Trage die fehlenden *possessive adjectives* ein.

Amy is going to a disco with ____________ friend Kirsty. ____________ boyfriend Bob is there, too. "____________ dress is lovely," he says to Amy. The song playing is by "Oasis". Tom loves ____________ music. He always plays ____________ songs at home and annoys ____________ parents. Amy listens to ____________ CDs sometimes. But ____________ favourite singer is Robbie Williams. They are dancing but the music is too loud. "____________ ears hurt," says Kirsty, "and ____________ feet are sore".

Fast lane

Übersetze die unterstrichenen Teile der Sätze ins Englische.

✔ = richtig ✘ = falsch

1 Tom bekommt einen Fußball <u>zu</u> *(for)* <u>seinem Geburtstag</u>.

____

<u>Seine Schwester</u> gibt ihm ein Buch.

____

2 Mrs Nunn räumt <u>ihren Bus</u> jeden Abend auf.

____

3 Adam versteckt <u>seine Bonbons</u> unter <u>seinem Schreibtisch</u>.

____

Sie liegen auf <u>seinem Englischbuch</u>.

____

4 Der arme Vogel hat <u>sich den Flügel</u> *(wing)* gebrochen.

___

5 Kleine Kinder tragen <u>ihre Schultaschen</u> *(school bag)* auf <u>dem Rücken</u> *(back)*, weil sie sehr schwer sind.

___

___

6 Kirsty packt <u>ihre Tasche</u>.

___

Weniger als 7 Punkte? Wenn ja, arbeite bitte Kapitel 2 B nochmals durch! max. 10

C Die Demonstrativpronomen

❶ – Who is **that** man over there?
– My English teacher.

❷ **Those** boys over there are in my class.

❸ – Ah, Tom, is **this** your mother?
– Yes, Miss Jones.

❹ Look at **these** tests. They are not very good, I'm afraid.

dieser – diese   jener – jene

- *This* (Singular) und *these* (Plural) verwenden wir bei nahe liegenden Dingen.
- *That* (Singular) und *those* (Plural) verwenden wir bei weiter entfernten Dingen.

Exercise 4

Füge jeweils die fehlende Form, Singular oder Plural, hinzu.

1 this flower, *these* flowers

2 __________ tree, those trees

3 __________ plant, these plants

4 that apple, __________ apples

5 this orange, __________ oranges

6 __________ potato, those potatoes

7 __________ banana, these bananas

8 that tomato, __________ tomatoes

Fast lane

Setze jeweils ein Demonstrativpronomen ein.

✔ = richtig ✘ = falsch

1 – Is *this* your dog here? ✔

– No, *that* is my dog over there. ✔

2 – Who is __________ man over there?

– Which man? Oh, __________ man. __________ is Mr Carter.

3 Which shoes do you think I should buy, __________ blue ones here or __________ red ones over there?

4 __________ sweets I'm eating are great!

5 – Look here, boys and girls. I've got __________ test. Whose is it?

– __________ is my test, Miss Jones.

– No, Tom. __________ isn't your test. __________ is your test over there. But isn't __________ your writing, Amy? I think __________ is your test.

– No, Miss Jones. __________ is not my test. __________ is my test. I have it in my hand.

Weniger als 10 Punkte? Wenn ja, arbeite Kapitel 2 C nochmals durch.

max. 14

Vokabelübungen 2 • Alltag und Schule

Crazy, crazy

Sieh dir das Bild an.
Es sind viele Sachen zu sehen, die alle mit dem Buchstaben **C** anfangen.
Schreibe sie unten auf und schreibe dann die Pluralform dazu.

Hast du alle 15 Sachen gefunden? Schreibe sie hier auf:

cake, ____________________

Hidden sentences

Schau dir die Bilder an und überlege, wie die abgebildeten Dinge auf Englisch heißen. Lasse dann die durchgestrichenen Buchstaben weg und ergänze die vorgegebenen Buchstaben. Die neuen Wörter ergeben einen Satz, wenn du alles richtig gemacht hast.

1  ~~MO~~

2 T +  ~~AD~~

3 WA +  ~~CR~~

4 

5 T +  ~~AD~~

6  ~~E~~ + K

7  ~~N~~ + KY

8  ~~A~~ + ES

9  ~~PL~~ ~~NE~~

10 

11 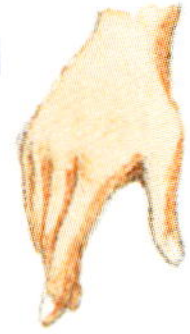 ~~H~~

12 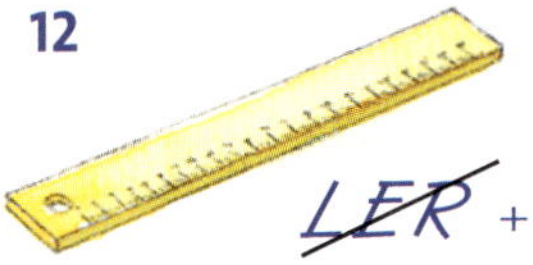 ~~LER~~ + NS

13 ~~L~~ E = A 

~~TURN~~ + ER

14 I +  ~~ABLE~~

Your sentence:

____

3 Der Artikel

A Der bestimmte Artikel *the*

B Der unbestimmte Artikel *a/an*

A Der bestimmte Artikel *the*

❶ **The dogs** in Oak Lane all play with Spooky.
❷ Miss Jones lives in **the old house** at **the end** of the road.

- Die Schreibweise des bestimmten Artikels bleibt immer dieselbe: *the*
- Die Aussprache dagegen ändert sich:
  Wenn das Wort direkt hinter dem Artikel mit einem Konsonanten beginnt, wird das *e* in *the* wie das **e** in „Jung**e**“ ausgesprochen [ðə]:
  the road   the dogs
- Beginnt das Wort hinter dem bestimten Artikel mit einem Vokal, musst du das *e* in *the* wie das **ie** in „L**ie**be” aussprechen [ðiː]:
  the old houses   the end

▷ **Der bestimmte Artikel steht nicht**

- vor Straßennamen:

in Oak Lane	*im Eichenweg*

- bei Bezeichnungen für Verkehrsmittel:

by train	*mit dem Zug*

- bei Bezeichnungen für bestimmte Gebäude bzw. Ortsangaben:

in hospital	*im Krankenhaus*
to school	*zur Schule*
in town	*in der Innenstadt*

- vor Bezeichnungen für Mahlzeiten als Zeitangabe:

after breakfast	*nach dem Frühstück*
before lunch	*vor dem Mittagessen*
during tea	*während des Abendbrots*

- vor *most* im Sinne von „die meisten":
  most children ... *die meisten Kinder ...*

▷ **Der bestimmte Artikel steht**
- vor Bezeichnungen für Musikinstrumente und technische Geräte (wie Radio); in Verbindung mit dem Verb *listen to*:
  listen to the radio *Radio hören*
  practise the piano *Klavier üben*

Exercise 1

Unterstreiche den bestimmten Artikel, bei dem du das *e* wie das **ie** in „L**ie**be" aussprechen musst [ðiː].

the airport; the aunt; the bottle; the cat; the CD; the egg; the English book; the exercise; the flower; the garden; the hospital; the house; the ice cream; the invitation; the jeans; the new school; the old town; the CD player; the taxi driver; the uncle.

Exercise 2

Setze den bestimmten Artikel nur dann ein, wenn es nötig ist.

1 Kirsty doesn't live in ________ Oak Lane. She lives in the white house at ________ end of ________ Cherry Tree Road.

2 ________ most/Most of ________ boys at ________ Green Park School like ________ football, but a lot of ________ girls think that ________ basketball or ________ volleyball is more fun.

3 – Do you go to ________ school by ________ bus or by ________ train?
– Well, I go by ________ taxi. ________ taxi/Taxi belongs to my dad, you see.

4 – Should we go to ________ town today? ________ film/Film about the Eskimos is on at ________ cinema in ________ Station Road.
– Yes, OK. We can go by ________ bike.

B Der unbestimmte Artikel *a/an*

❶ Adam, eat **an apple** and **a banana**, not all those sweets.
❷ Bob is **a child** and Mr Parker is **an adult**.

▶ Wenn das Wort direkt hinter dem unbestimmten Artikel mit einem Konsonanten beginnt, dann musst du *a* verwenden: *a banana; a child.*

▶ Beginnt das Wort hinter dem unbestimmten Artikel mit einem Vokal, musst du *an* verwenden: *an apple; an adult.*

▷ **Der unbestimmte Artikel steht**

- bei Berufsangaben:
  Mr Bunn **is a baker** *(ist Bäcker)* and Mr Parker **is an engineer** *(ist Ingenieur).*

- bei bestimmten Krankheiten und Zuständen:
  Amy's **got a cold** *(ist erkältet)* and she **has a headache** *(hat Kopfschmerzen)*, too.

- in folgenden Wendungen:

be in a hurry	*in Eile sein*
have a bath/shower/wash	*baden/duschen/(sich) waschen*
ride a bike	*Fahrrad fahren*
What a pity!	*Wie schade!*
for a long time	*lange (Zeit)*
a quarter to ... /past ...	*(ein) Viertel vor ... / nach ...*

Exercise 3

Setze *a* oder *an* vor den Wörtern ein.

_a_ man; _an_ old book; _an_ accident; _an_ address; _a_ bag;
_a_ cake; _a_ DVD player; _a_ dirty shoe; _an_ egg; _an_ English book;
_an_ expensive T-shirt; _a_ family; _a_ flat; _a_ guitar; _a_ hand;
_a_ hotel; _an_ hour; _an_ idea; _a_ CD; _a_ magazine; _a_ mistake;
_a_ noise; _an_ old car; _an_ orange; _a_ pen; _a_ pet; _a_ question;
_an_ uncle; _an_ underground train; _an_ uniform; _an_ untidy room;
_a_ village; _a_ wall; _a_ year; _a_ yellow apple; _a_ zoo

Fast lane

Übersetze die unterstrichenen Teile der Sätze ins Englische.

✔ = richtig ✘ = falsch

1 Mrs Nunn ist Busfahrerin.

2 Bob hat Kopfschmerzen und Adam ist erkältet.

3 Tom ist so langsam. Wir sind in Eile.

4 Kann Mr Parker Fahrrad fahren?

5 Wir warten immer lange Zeit auf den Bus.

6 Kirsty hat eine Uniform, aber sie zieht sie nie an.

7 Es ist jetzt Viertel vor acht.

8 Wie schade! Der Fernseher ist kaputt.

9 Tom duscht gerade.

10 Amy will Lehrerin werden, wenn sie groß ist.

Weniger als 8 Punkte? Wenn ja, arbeite bitte Kapitel 3 B nochmals durch! max. 11

4 Zahlen

A Kardinalzahlen

B Ordinalzahlen

A Kardinalzahlen

1	one	5	five	9	nine
2	two	6	six	10	ten
3	three	7	seven	11	eleven
4	four	8	eight	12	twelve

▶ Kardinalzahlen beantworten die Frage „wie viel ...?“

13	thirteen	17	seventeen
14	fourteen	18	eighteen
15	fifteen	19	nineteen
16	sixteen		

▶ Um die Zahlen von 13 bis 19 zu bilden, nehmen wir die Zehner plus den Einer, genau wie im Deutschen.

20	twenty	26	twenty-six	50	fifty
21	twenty-one	27	twenty-seven	60	sixty
22	twenty-two	28	twenty-eight	70	seventy
23	twenty-three	29	twenty-nine	80	eighty
24	twenty-four	30	thirty	90	ninety
25	twenty-five	40	forty		

▶ Die restlichen Zahlen bis 100 werden in der gleichen Reihenfolge gesprochen, wie sie geschrieben werden.

100	a/one hundred
200	two hundred
210	two hundred **and** ten
225	two hundred **and** twenty-five
1000	a/one thousand
2000	two thousand
2010	two thousand **and** ten
2225	two thousand two hundred **and** twenty-five

▶ Bei Zahlen über 100 stellen wir das Wörtchen *and* vor die letzte Zahl der Reihe.

Exercise 1

Schreibe die Zahlen aus.

14 _ _ _ _ _ _ _ _

89 _ _ _ _ _ _ - _ _ _ _

11 _ _ _ _ _ _

52 _ _ _ _ _ - _ _ _

15 _ _ _ _ _ _ _

33 _ _ _ _ _ _ - _ _ _ _ _

19 _ _ _ _ _ _ _ _

98 _ _ _ _ _ _ - _ _ _ _ _

12 _ _ _ _ _ _

45 _ _ _ _ _ - _ _ _ _

215 _ _ _   _ _ _ _ _ _ _

_ _ _   _ _ _ _ _ _ _

Exercise 2

Zähle die Dinge, die überall in Adams Zimmer herumliegen. Schreibe in Worten auf, wie viele er von den verschiedenen Sachen hat.

Adam has got:

__________ radio,	__________ sweets,
__________ books,	__________ CDs,
__________ pens,	__________ posters,
__________ toy cars, and	__________ CD player.

Exercise 3

Schreibe die Zahlen in Worten auf.

1 He lives at number 378 City Road.

three hundred and seventy-eight

2 My phone number is Epping 690631.

six –

3 The score *(Ergebnis)* is Manchester 1 : Liverpool 0.

4 I'd like to go to the Olympic Games in 2008.

5 The year 1996 was *(war)* the year of the last Olympic Games in the last century.

6 There are 1386 pupils at our school.

Fast lane

Beantworte diese Fragen. Schreibe die Zahlen bitte voll aus.

✔ = richtig ✘ = falsch

1 How many days are there in a year?

three hundred and sixty-five ✔

2 How much is 35 and 46?

____

3 How many days are there in July?

____

4 How many years are there in a century?

____

5 How many months are there in a year?

____

6 How many legs does a spider *(Spinne)* have?

____

7 How many grams are there in a kilogram?

____

8 How much is 27 and 23?

____

9 How many kilometres are there in a marathon run?

____

Weniger als 6 Punkte? Wenn ja, arbeite bitte Kapitel 4 A nochmals durch. max. 8

B Ordinalzahlen

the first	–	1**st**	the twenty-first	–	21**st**
the second	–	2**nd**	the twenty-second	–	22**nd**
the third	–	3**rd**	the twenty-third	–	23**rd**
the fourth	–	4**th**	the twenty-fourth	–	24**th**
the fifth	–	5th	the thirtieth	–	30th
the sixth	–	6th	the fortieth	–	40th
the seventh	–	7th	the fiftieth	–	50th
the eighth	–	8th	the sixtieth	–	60th
the ninth	–	9th	the eightieth	–	80th
the tenth	–	10th	the ninetieth	–	90th
the twentieth	–	20th	the hundredth	–	100th

▶ Ordinalzahlen beantworten die Frage „die/der/das wievielte ...?".

Exercise 4

Schreibe die gesuchten Buchstaben auf.
Hast du alles richtig gemacht, ergeben die gefunden Buchstaben einen Satz.

1 The third letter of the tenth month of the year. [T]
2 The second letter of the fourth day of the week. [ ]
3 The fourth letter of the fourth month of the year. [ ]
4 The sixth letter of the third day of the week. [ ]
5 The third letter of the fifth day of the week. [ ]
6 The fifth letter of the eighth month of the year. [ ]
7 The seventh letter of the twelfth month of the year. [ ]
8 The seventh letter of the sixth day of the week. [ ]
9 The sixth letter of the third day of the week. [ ]
10 The eighth letter of the second month of the year. [ ]

Dein Satz: T ______________________________

Fast lane

Schreibe auf, an wievielter Stelle die vorgegebenen Buchstaben im Alphabet stehen.

✔ = richtig ✘ = falsch

1	E	is *fifth*.	7	C	is ______.	✔
2	N	is ______.	8	H	is ______.	
3	G	is ______.	9	W	______.	
4	L	is ______.	10	O	______.	
5	I	is ______.	11	R	______.	
6	S	is ______.	12	T	______.	

Weniger als 8 Punkte? Wenn ja, arbeite bitte Kapitel 4 B nochmals durch. max 11

5 Uhrzeiten und Datum

A Uhrzeiten

B Datum

A Uhrzeiten

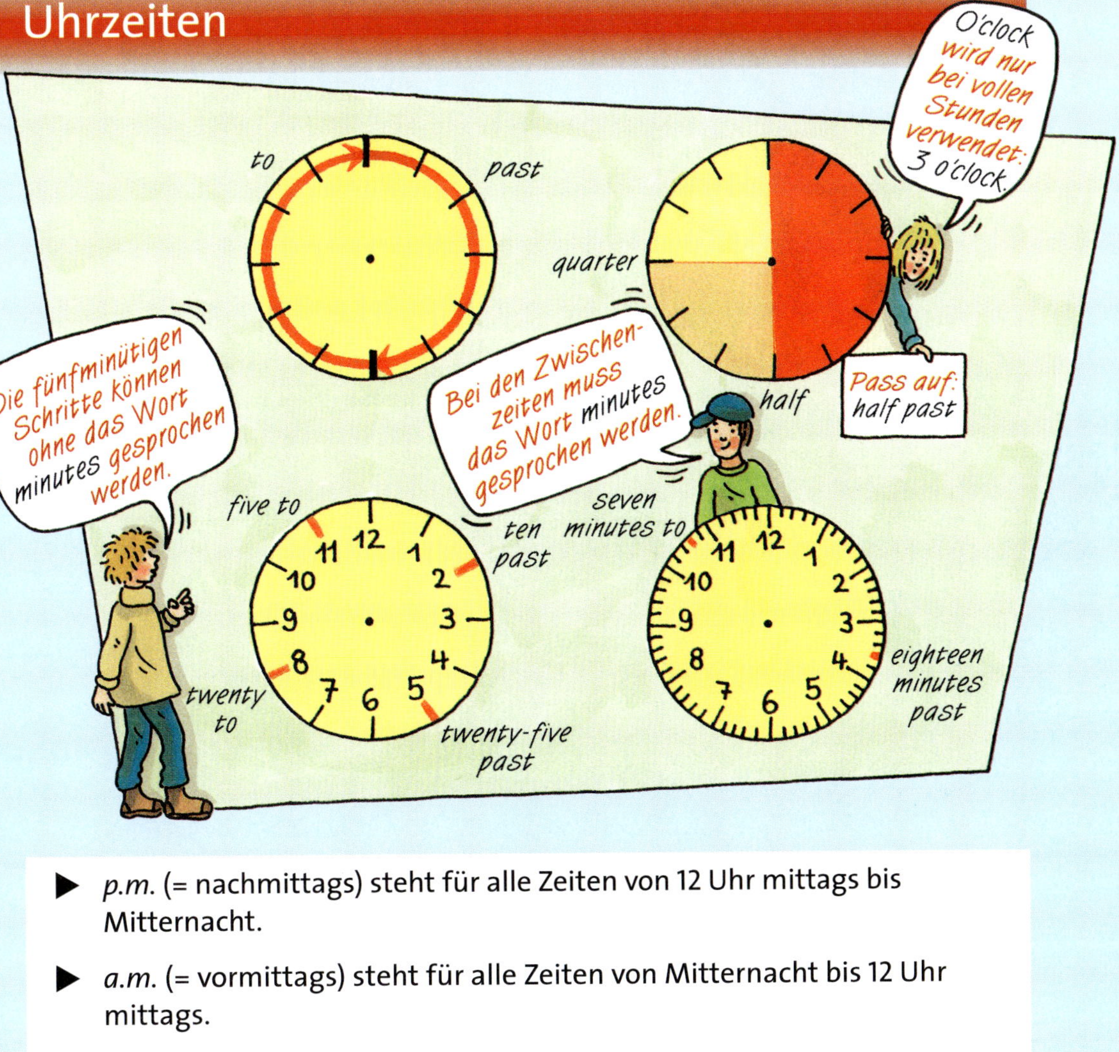

- *p.m.* (= nachmittags) steht für alle Zeiten von 12 Uhr mittags bis Mitternacht.
- *a.m.* (= vormittags) steht für alle Zeiten von Mitternacht bis 12 Uhr mittags.
- Man kann *o'clock* und *a.m./p.m.* nicht gleichzeitig benutzen.
- *Past* (= nach) wird nur für die ersten 30 Minuten nach einer vollen Stunde verwendet.

▶ Für die 29 Minuten vor der nächsten vollen Stunde verwenden wir *to* (= vor).

9.10	ten	**past** nine	9.31	twenty-nine	**to** ten
9.15	quarter	**past** nine	9.45	quarter	**to** ten
9.30	half	**past** nine	9.50	ten	**to** ten

▷ Man muss nicht unbedingt *past* und *to* verwenden, sondern kann auch – ähnlich wie im Deutschen – sagen:

2.04	2.15	2.30	2.52
two-o-four	two fifteen	two thirty	two fifty-two

▷ Aufpassen: **at** ten o'clock – **um** zehn Uhr
about ten o'clock – **gegen** zehn Uhr

Exercise 1

Male die folgenden Uhrzeiten auf.

1 half past two
2 quarter to seven
3 ten to six
4 twenty-five past one
5 quarter past ten
6 twenty-three minutes past twelve
7 seven minutes to four
8 half past eleven

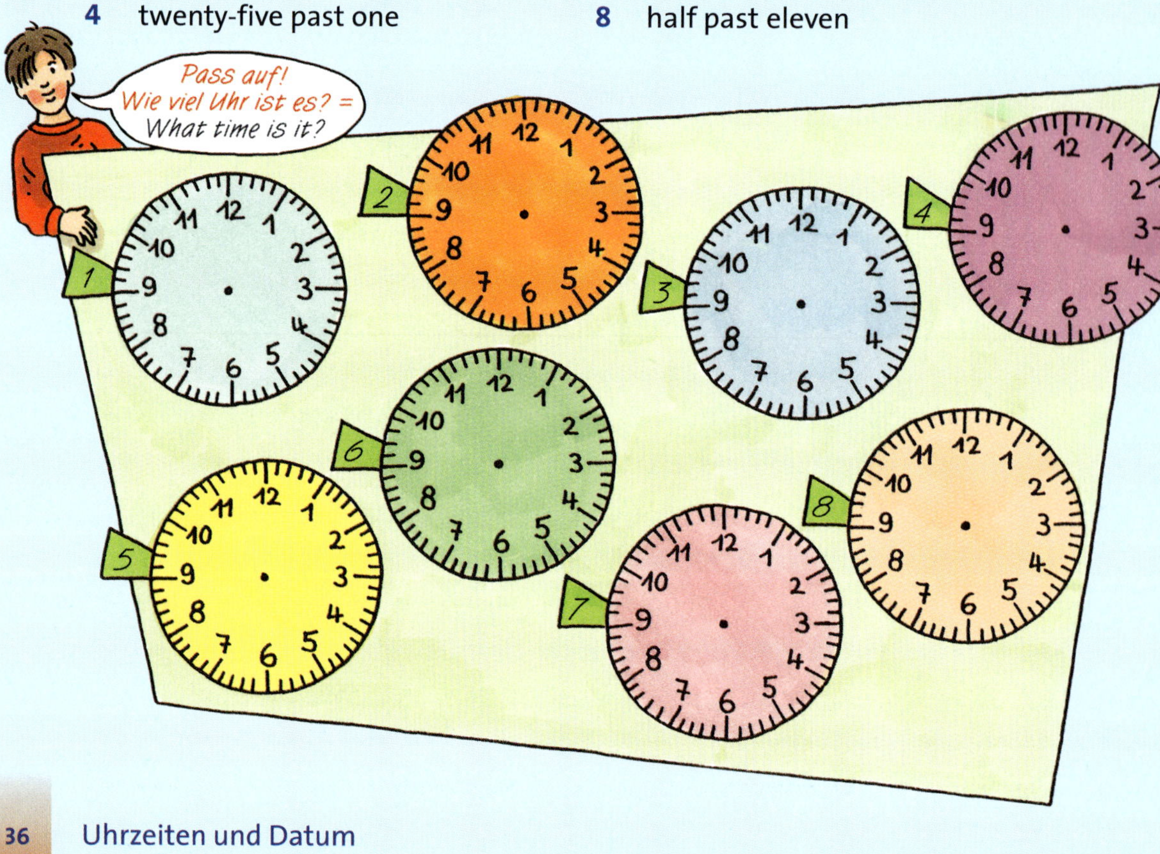

Exercise 2

Schreibe die richtigen Uhrzeiten unter die Uhren.

1 seven o'clock

2 ______

3 ______

4 ______

5 ______

6 ______

7 ______

8 ______

Fast lane

Sieh dir die Abfahrtszeiten an und vervollständige die Sätze unten.
Verwende *past* und *to*.

✔ = richtig ✘ = falsch

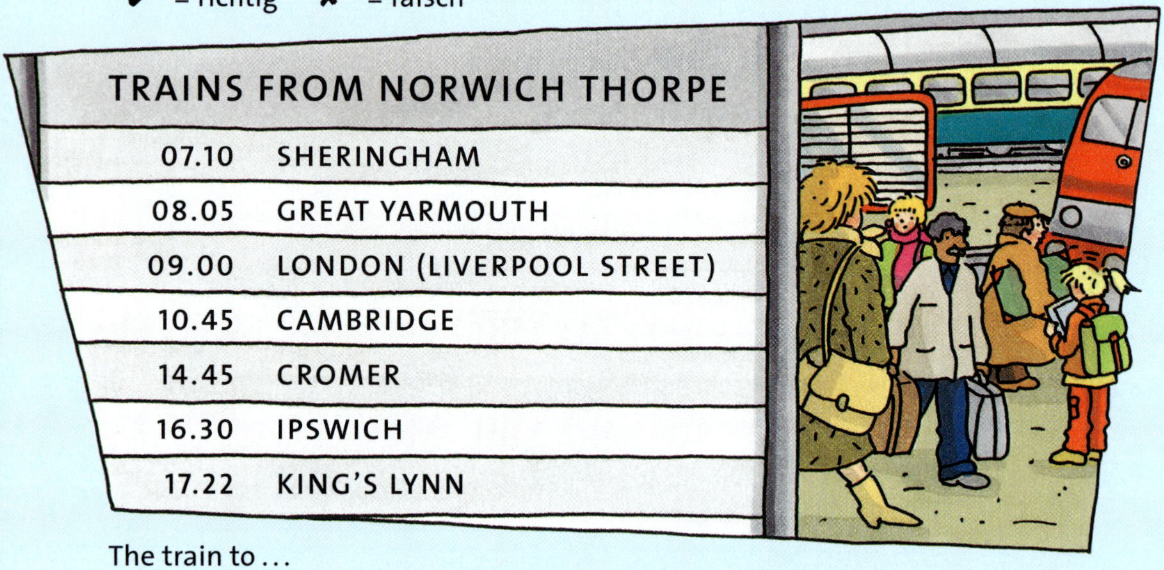

The train to …

1 … Sheringham leaves Norwich at *ten past seven* a.m. ✔

2 … Great Yarmouth goes at ______________ a.m.

3 … London leaves at ______________ a.m.

4 … Cambridge is at ______________ a.m.

5 … Cromer goes ______________ p.m.

6 … Ipswich ______________ p.m.

7 … King's Lynn ______________ p.m.

Weniger als 4 Punkte? Wenn ja, arbeite bitte Kapitel 5 A nochmals durch. max. 6

B Datum

January	April	July	October
February	May	August	November
March	June	September	December

▶ Daten werden anders geschrieben, als sie ausgesprochen werden:

wir schreiben	wir sagen
on 29th March	"on the twenty-ninth of March" oder "on March the twenty-ninth"
on 4th July	"on the fourth of July" oder "on July the fourth"

Exercise 3

Bob liest die nächsten Fußballspieltermine vor. Wie spricht er die Daten aus?

1 June 12 — *the twelfth of June*

2 April 1 — ____________________

3 August 23 — ____________________

4 January 31 — ____________________

5 December 20 — ____________________

6 November 3 — ____________________

Exercise 4

Wie werden diese gesprochenen Daten geschrieben?

on the twenty-third of March — 1 *on 23rd March*

on the thirteenth of May — 2 ____________________

on the seventh of September — 3 ____________________

on the second of October — 4 ____________________

on the first of February — 5 ____________________

on the twenty-ninth of May — 6 ____________________

Fast lane

Amy liest Geburtstagstermine aus Mrs Cobbs Geburtstagskalender vor.

Schreib auf, was sie sagt.

✔ = richtig ✘ = falsch

1 Adam's birthday is on *the ninth of January*. ✔

2 Tom's is on ____________________.

3 Miss Jones' is ____________________.

4 Kirsty's ____________________.

5 Colin's ____________________.

6 Mrs Cobb's ____________________.

7 My birthday ____________________.

And when is *your* birthday?

My birthday is ____________________.

Weniger als 5 Punkte? Wenn ja, arbeite bitte Kapitel 5 B nochmals durch.

max. 7

6 Das Verb *be* – Gegenwart

A Die Gegenwart von *be*

❶ Bob Parker: I **am** a pupil at Green Park School.
❷ Green Park School **is** in Kingston.
❸ Bob **is** captain of Green Park School football team.
❹ They **are** Bob's friends.

▶ In den Sätzen oben steht das Verb *be* allein. Es ist also ein Vollverb.

▷ Die Gegenwart von *be* hat folgende Formen:

I	am
you	are
he, she, it	is
we, you, they	are

Exercise 1

Setze die richtige Form von *be* ein. Benutze aber bitte nur die Langform.

My name ___is___ Bob Parker. I _________ a pupil at Green Park School in Kingston. Kingston _________ a town near London. My friends _________ Tom and Amy Cobb. They _________ pupils at Green Park, too. I _________ captain of the Green Park football team, and Tom ________ the goalkeeper *(Torwart)*.

He ________ quite good, but I ________ the star. And Amy? She ________ great. She ________ also my girlfriend and head (*Leiterin*) of my fan club.

B Die Verneinung

❶ Amy: **I'm not** Adam's girlfriend. I'm Bob's girlfriend.
❷ **Tom is not** the captain of the school football team. That's Bob.
❸ **Tom and Adam aren't** brothers. They are friends.

▶ In verneinten englischen Sätzen funktioniert *be* genau wie „sein" im Deutschen ❶ ❷ ❸.

▷ Die Verneinung von *be* hat folgende Formen:

	Langform	Kurzform
I	am not	'm not
you	are	not 're not/aren't
he, she, it	is not	's not/isn't
we, you, they	are not	're not/aren't

Exercise 2

Die Sätze sind alle sachlich falsch.
Verneine sie mit der Lang- oder Kurzform und du bekommst richtige Aussagen.

1 – London is in Scotland.
– No, that's wrong.
London *is not/isn't* in Scotland.

2 – Hamburgers are very good for you.
– Oh, no. They ________ at all good for you.

3 – The Rhine is the longest river in Europe.
– That's not right. The Rhine ________ the longest river in Europe.

4 – Hamsters are dangerous animals.

– That's silly. Hamsters ________________ dangerous.

5 – Tom is the captain of the football team.

– No, that's wrong. Bob is the captain of the football team and Tom ________________ captain of the team.

6 – You are late again, Tom.

– No, Sir. I ________________ late. It's only 10 o'clock.

Fast lane

Ergänze die Sätze durch eine Verneinung.

✔ = richtig ✘ = falsch

1 Kirsty is Amy's girlfriend, but she _is not/isn't_ Adam's girlfriend. ✔

2 England is big, but it ____________________ the biggest country in Europe.

3 Hamsters are small animals, but elephants ____________________ small animals.

4 The Cobbs' dog ____________________ called Coco. It's called Spooky.

5 Cars are fast, but they ____________________ faster than planes.

6 Tom is good at sport, but he ____________________ good at maths.

7 Vegetables are good for you, but sweets ____________________ good for you.

8 The weather is warm in summer, but it ____________________ warm in winter.

Weniger als 5 Punkte? Wenn ja, arbeite bitte Kapitel 6 A und 6 B nochmals durch! max. 7

C Fragen

❶ **Are you** in the football team, Adam? – No, **I'm not**.
❷ **Is Tom** at Green Park School? – Yes, **he is**.
❸ **Are Amy and Kirsty** sisters? – No, **they aren't**.

▶ In Fragen funktioniert *be* genau wie „sein" im Deutschen ❶ ❷ ❸.

Exercise 3

Bilde Fragen.

1 Amy is a good pupil.

Is Amy a good pupil?

2 Bob is Amy's brother.

______________________________?

3 Tom is the captain this year.

______________________________?

4 Amy and Bob are good friends.

______________________________?

5 Amy is Kirsty's best friend.

______________________________?

6 I am in the team for the next match.

______________________________?

Fast lane

Stelle Fragen, zu denen die vorgegebenen Antworten passen.

✔ = richtig ✘ = falsch

1 *Is Tom Cobb* in Mr Wood's class? (Tom Cobb) ✔

– No, he's in Miss Jones' class.

2 ______________ at King's School? (the Cobb children)

– No, they're at Green Park.

3 ______________________ a friendly teacher? (Old Carter)

– No, but Miss Jones is a friendly teacher.

4 ______________________ the Clarkes' cat? (Spooky)

– Oh, no. He's the Cobbs' dog.

5 ______________________ next? (I)

– No, I think Bob is next.

6 ______________________ in France? (Hamburg and Cologne)

– No, they are in Germany.

7 ______________________ a lorry driver? (Mrs Nunn)

– No, she's a bus driver.

8 ______________________ Adam's girlfriend? (Amy)

– No, she's Bob's girlfriend.

Weniger als 5 Punkte? Wenn ja, arbeite bitte Kapitel 6 A und 6 C nochmals durch! max. 7

Super fast lane

Bilde jeweils zwei Sätze wie vorgegeben.

✔ = richtig ✘ = falsch

1 (Berlin/a city in England)

Is Berlin a city in England? ✔

No, *Berlin isn't a city in England.* ✔

2 (Tom/Kirsty's brother)

______________________?

No, ______________________

3 (London/a small town)

______________________?

No, ______________________

4 (Miss Jones/Mr Carter's friend)

______________________?

No, ______________________

5 (Mr Carter/a good teacher)

____ ?

No, ____

6 (Kirsty/Tom's girlfriend)

____ ?

No, ____

7 (Harry Potter's aunt/nice)

____ ?

No, ____

8 (Green Park/a bad school)

____ ?

No, ____

Weniger als 10 Punkte? Wenn ja, arbeite bitte Kapitel 6 A bis 6 C nochmals durch!

D Befehle

Miss Jones: **Don't be** so silly, Tom. **Be quiet**, please.

▶ Bei der Befehlsform setzt du einfach *be* bzw. *don't be* an den Anfang des Satzes:

Don't	be	so silly,	Tom.
	Be	quiet,	please.

Exercise 4

Der arme Adam Clarke macht anscheinend gar nichts richtig.
Sage bitte Adam mit *be/don't be*, wie er sein und nicht sein soll.

1 so noisy/quiet

Don't be so noisy, Adam. *Be quiet*, please.

2 so lazy/helpful *(hilfsbereit)*

_______________ so lazy, Adam. _______________, please.

3 so naughty *(ungezogen)*/good

_______________ so naughty, Adam. _______________, please.

4 so silly/sensible *(vernünftig)*

_______________, Adam. _______________, please.

5 so careless *(unvorsichtig)*/more careful

____ .

E Die Kurzform von *be*

❶ Bob **is** a pupil at Green Park School, and Tom**'s** a pupil at Green Park School, too.
❷ I **am** not a very good football player, but I**'m** quite a good singer.
❸ We**'re** good friends.

▶ In Unterhaltungen und privaten Briefen/Postkarten/E-Mails verwenden wir die Kurzform.

▷

	Langform	Kurzform
I	am	'm
you	are	're
he, she, it	is	's
we, you, they	are	're

▷ Hier sind weitere wichtige Kurzformen, die du dir merken musst:

here's	= here is	**how's?**	= how is?
that's	= that is	**there's**	= there is
what's?	= what is?	**where's?**	= where is?
who's?	= who is?		

Exercise 5

Unterstreiche die Kurzformen in diesem Text.

It's Saturday, and Tom and Amy are waiting for their friends. They're having a party. "Where's the coke?" asks Amy. "Tom, there's no coke." "Yes, there is," says Tom. "Twelve bottles. They're in the kitchen. That's enough. I always buy it at Smith's. You know, the shop in Queen's Street. Coke's cheap there." "Oh," says Amy, "you're just like dad. He's always looking for cheap things, too." "What's wrong with that?" says Tom. "We're not rich!"

Fast lane

Die folgende Unterhaltung klingt sehr unnatürlich, weil nur die Langform verwendet wird.
Benutze die Kurzform, um den Dialog lockerer und freundlicher zu machen.

✔ = richtig ✘ = falsch

Tom (Mr Carter is not) Mr Carter's not so good. ✔

(He is) ____________ very strict *(streng)*.

(I am) ____________ glad when maths is over.

Amy Oh, come on, Tom. (Old Carter is) ____________ OK.

(You are) ____________ lazy, (that is) ____________ all.

(You are) ____________ often late for his lessons, and

(you are) ____________ cheeky *(frech)* to him, too.

(I am) ____________ not surprised *(überrascht)*

that (he is) ____________ sometimes angry with you.

Bob Yes, (Amy is) ____________ right, Tom.

(You are not) ____________ very interested in his lessons.

And (you are not) ____________ very good a maths either.

Weniger als 7 Punkte? Wenn ja, arbeite bitte Kapitel 6 F nochmals durch! max 10

7 Das Verb *have* – Gegenwart

A Die Gegenwart von *have*

B Die Verneinung

C Fragen

D *have got*

E Die Verneinung von *have got*

F Fragen mit *have got*

A Die Gegenwart von *have*

❶ **I** always **have** breakfast before I go to school.
❷ **Bob** always **has** a shower after football matches.
❸ **We have** a great holiday in France every summer.

▷ In Aussagesätzen hat die Gegenwart von *have* folgende Formen:

	Langform	Kurzform		Langform	Kurzform
I	have	I've	we	have	we've
you	have	you've	you	have	you've
he, she, it	has	–	they	have	they've

Exercise 1

Setze die Langform der Gegenwart von *have* ein.

On Wednesdays, Amy ___has___ maths in the morning, then she __________ history. At eleven o'clock the whole school __________ a break *(Pause)*. Then her class __________ English. At lunchtime, Amy meets her friends and they all __________ lunch together. In the afternoon, she __________ sport and then her music lesson. "We ___________ a very busy day on Wednesdays," she tells her mother.

B Die Verneinung

❶ Amy **doesn't have** cornflakes for breakfast.
❷ We **don't have** Maths on Tuesdays.

▶ Wir bilden verneinte Sätze mit *do/does not*, genau wie bei anderen Vollverben ❶ ❷.

Exercise 2

Bilde verneinte Sätze mit der Lang- oder Kurzform wie vorgegeben.

1 Amy has tea in the afternoon.
Amy *does not/doesn't have* tea in the afternoon.

2 Mr and Mrs Cobb have a car.
Mr and Mrs Cobb ______________________________ a car.

3 Mrs Nunn has a lot of time.
Mrs Nunn ______________________________ a lot of time.

4 Kirsty has milk for breakfast.
Kirsty ______________________________ milk for breakfast.

5 Bob and Tom have a good time at the youth club every week.
Bob and Tom ______________________________ a good time at the youth club every week.

6 We have a Chinese meal on Saturdays.
We ______________________________ a Chinese meal on Saturdays.

7 I have a shower every morning.
I ______________________________ a shower every morning.

Fast lane

Setze die verneinte Form von *have* ein.

At the weekend Tom doesn't have school, which means he ______________ maths and he ______________ history. "I ______________ school today!," says Tom, "I ______________ anything to do! It's great."
"You ______________ school today, Tom, and you ______________ any homework, but your grandparents need a few things from the shop. They ______________ much food at home and they ______________ time to do the shopping."

Weniger als 6 Punkte? Wenn ja, arbeite bitte Kapitel 7 A und 7 B nochmals durch! max. 8

C Fragen

❶ **Do** you **have** coffee for breakfast? – No, I don't.
❷ **Does** Adam **have** a holiday in France every summer? – Yes, he does.

▶ Wir bilden Fragen mit *do/does*, genau wie bei anderen Vollverben ❶ ❷.

Exercise 3

Bilde Fragen wie in den folgenden Beispielsätzen vorgegeben.

1 Amy has milk with her tea.
Does Amy have milk with her tea?

2 Mr and Mrs Cobb have lunch together every day.
Do Mr and Mrs Cobb have lunch together every day?

3 Tom Cobb has football practice every week.
______________ football practice every week?

4 Kirsty has dancing lessons on Thursdays.
______________ dancing lessons on Thursdays?

5 Amy has a terrible cold.

__________________________________ a terrible cold?

6 Tom and Bob have a shower after football practice.

__________________________________ a shower after football practice?

7 Adam has sweets for lunch today.

__________________________________ sweets for lunch today?

8 I have tea at six o'clock.

__________________________________ tea at six o'clock?

Fast lane

Setze die richtige Form von *have* in die Aussage- und Fragesätze ein.
Achte auf das Satzzeichen am Ende des Satzes.

✔ = richtig ✘ = falsch

Bob _____________________ any time this afternoon?

Amy Yes, I _____________________ plenty of time.

Bob Good, then we can play tennis. _____________________ tennis shoes?

Amy No. _____________________ a pair for me?

Bob Yes, I _____________________ two pairs. You can wear the blue ones.

Amy Great, thanks. _____________________ time for two games?

Bob No, because I _____________________ a music lesson at five-thirty.

Amy _____________________ 50 pence? I'd like a drink before we play.

Bob OK, Amy, let's _____________________ something to drink first.

Weniger als 6 Punkte? Wenn ja, arbeite bitte Kapitel 7 A und 7 C nochmals durch! max. 9

Super fast lane

Übersetze die unterstrichenen Satzteile.

✔ = richtig ✘ = falsch

1 Spooky badet nicht jeden Tag.

___

2 Hast du Zeit?

___

3 Bob hat eine gute Idee.

___

4 Frühstückt Mr Clarke jeden Morgen?

___

5 Hat Bob zwei Paar Tennisschuhe?

___

6 Amy hat keine Tennisschuhe.

___

7 Mrs Nunn hat keinen Garten.

___

8 Hat Adam eine Schwester?

___

9 Ich habe keinen Farbfernseher.

___

10 Haben Mr und Mrs Clarke ein Auto?

___

Weniger als 7 Punkte? Wenn ja, arbeite bitte Kapitel 7 A bis 7 C nochmals durch! max. 10

D *have got*

▶ Wenn *have* „besitzen“ bedeutet, wird *have* in der Gegenwart oft durch *have got* ersetzt, um diese Bedeutung zu betonen:

> Bob **has got** a new football.
> Bob hat/besitzt einen neuen Fußball.

▷ In Aussagesätzen mit *have got* sind die Formen die gleichen wie für *have*. Du findest sie auf Seite 47.

Exercise 4

Setze die Langform der Gegenwart von *have* ein. Benutze *have got*, wenn *have* eindeutig „besitzen“ bedeutet.

1 The Cobbs _have got_ a house. Amy and Tom ________________ a little dog called Spooky. Spooky always ________________ a lot of fun with the other dogs in Green Park. Sometimes they ________________ a race. And Amy always ________________ a good time with her friend Kirsty. When Spooky is dirty he ________________ a bath when they are at home again.
Amy and Tom ________________ a budgie, too. Its name is Tweets.

2 Tom always ________________ a super party on his birthday. Everybody ________________ a great time there. Tom always ________________ lots of cakes, coke and ice cream. But not this time. Poor Tom says he ________________ no money.

3 Mr and Mrs Parker ________________ a garden. They ________________ many flowers but they ________________ little time to work in the garden.

E Die Verneinung von *have got*

❶ I **haven't got** a dog.
❷ Amy **hasn't got** a football.
❸ Kirsty and Adam **haven't got** a dog.

▶ Mit *have got* bilden wir verneinte Sätze ohne das Hilfsverb *do* ❶ – ❸.

▷ Die Verneinung von *have got* hat folgende Formen:

	Langform	**Kurzform**
I, you	have not got	haven't got
he, she, it	has not got	hasn't got
we, you, they	have not got	haven't got

Exercise 5

Bilde verneinte Sätze mit der Lang- oder Kurzform.

1 Amy has got a new coat.
Amy *has not got/hasn't got* a new coat.

2 Tom Cobb has got a new bike.
Tom Cobb ______________________________ a new bike.

3 Tom and Amy have got lots of video games.
Tom and Amy ______________________________ lots of video games.

4 I have got a felt tip.
____

5 Adam has got a new cap.
____

6 The Parkers have got a swimming pool.
____

7 Kirsty has got a camcorder.
____

F Fragen mit *have got*

❶ **Has** Adam **got** a dog? – No, **he hasn't**.
❷ **Have** Mr and Mrs Cobb **got** a dog? – Yes, **they have**.

- Mit *have got* bilden wir Fragen ohne das Hilfsverb *do* ❶ ❷.
- Bei der Kurzantwort entfällt das Wörtchen *got* ❶ ❷.

Exercise 6

Bilde Fragesätze wie im folgenden Beispiel vorgegeben.

1 Tom and Amy have got a budgie.

Have Tom and Amy got a budgie?

Yes, they have.

2 Bob has got a football.

______________________________?

Yes, he has.

3 Kirsty has got a CD player.

______________________________?

Yes, she has.

4 Adam has got a blue cap.

______________________________?

Yes, he has.

5 Mr and Mrs Clarke have got a car.

______________________________?

Yes, they have.

6 Amy has got a kickboard.

______________________________?

Yes, she has.

8 Das Verb *do* – Gegenwart

A *Do* als Vollverb

B *Do* als Hilfsverb: die Verneinung

C *Do* als Hilfsverb: Fragen und Kurzantworten

D *Do* als Hilfsverb: die verneinte Befehlsform

E *Do* als Vollverb und Hilfsverb

A *Do* als Vollverb

❶ I always **do** my homework before I go to bed. *(erledigen)*
❷ She **does** what she wants. *(tun, machen)*

▷ In Aussagesätzen hat die Gegenwart von *do* folgende Formen:

I, you	do
he, she, it	does
we, you, they	do

Exercise 1

Setze die richtige Form von *do* in die Sätze ein.

1 Bob often ______________ sport on Saturdays.

2 Harry Potter sometimes ______________ magic tricks.

3 When Mrs Cobb is ill, the children ______________ the housework.

4 At school, Kirsty ______________ a test every month.

5 Spooky and Coco ______________ tricks sometimes.

6 In Britain, small children ______________ their homework at school.

B *Do* als Hilfsverb: die Verneinung

❶ He **does not** play handball.
❷ They **do not** go to King's School.

▶ Bei der Verneinung erscheint das *-s* für die 3. Person Singular nicht mehr beim Vollverb, sondern nur beim Hilfsverb *does*. ❶
Das Vollverb steht immer im Infinitiv. ❶ ❷

▷ Wir bilden die Verneinung mit *do* wie folgt:

	Langform	**Kurzform**
I, you	do not	don't
he, she, it	does not	doesn't
we, you, they	do not	don't

Exercise 2

Die Sätze unten sind alle sachlich falsch.
Stelle sie richtig mit Hilfe der Angaben in Klammern.

1 Bob plays basketball. (football)

Bob _does not (doesn't)_ play basketball. He _plays_ football.

2 Mr Cobb works in London. (Kingston)

Mr Cobb ________________________ in London. He __________ in Kingston.

3 Mrs Nunn drives a train. (a bus)

Mrs Nunn __________________________ a train. She ____________ a bus.

4 Bob and Tom live in Ash St. (Oak Lane)

Bob and Tom __________________________ in Ash St.

They ___________ in Oak Lane.

5 Adam eats a lot of fruit. (sweets)

Adam __________________________ much fruit.

He ___________ a lot of sweets.

6 Mrs Clarke goes to the cinema with Miss Jones. (Mrs Carter)

Mrs Clarke ____

____

7 The children watch videos at the weekend. (play games)

The children ____

____.

Fast lane

Übersetze die unterstrichenen Teile der folgenden Sätze ins Englische.

✔ = richtig ✘ = falsch

1 Tom und Bob spielen nicht Handball.

____

2 Samstags gehen Kinder nicht zur Schule in Großbritannien.

____

3 Amy und Tom wohnen nicht in der Green Road.

____

4 Montags gehe ich nicht ins Kino.

____

5 Kirsty spielt nicht Fußball.

____

6 Sonntags macht ihr nicht eure Hausaufgaben.

____

Weniger als 4 Punkte? Wenn ja, arbeite bitte Kapitel 8 A und 8 B nochmals durch! max. 6

C *Do* als Hilfsverb: Fragen und Kurzantworten

do	Subjekt	Vollverb	andere Teile	Kurzantwort
Does	Bob	live	in Oak Lane, too?	Yes, **he does**.
Does	Adam	play	football?	No, **he doesn't**.
Do	we	like	Mr Carter?	No, **we don't**.
Do	they	go	to Green Park School?	Yes, **they do**.

▶ Genau wie bei der Verneinung heißt die Form des Hilfsverbs für die 3. Person Singular *does*. Auch hier steht das Vollverb immer im Infinitiv.

Aussage: Bob live**s** in Oak Lane, too.

Frage: Doe**s** Bob **live** in Oak Lane, too?

Exercise 3

Bilde Fragen mit *do/does* und schreibe die passende Kurzantwort dazu.

1 Bob thinks he is a great football player.

Does Bob think he is a great football player?

Yes, *he does*.

2 The children live in Oak Lane.

____________________ in Oak Lane?

Yes, they __________.

3 Adam likes Old Carter.

____________________ like Old Carter?

No, he __________.

4 Adam eats too many sweets.

____________________ too many sweets?

Yes, he __________.

5 Tom and Amy go to the cinema every Sunday.

____________________ to the cinema every Sunday?

No, __________.

6 Kirsty helps her mother a lot.

____.

Yes, ____________________.

7 Mr Carter walks to school.

____.

No, ____________________.

8 Green Park wins every football match.

____.

No, ____________________.

Fast lane

Übersetze die unterstrichenen Teile der folgenden Sätze ins Englische.

✔ = richtig ✘ = falsch

1 Wohnt Kirsty auch in Oak Lane?

____.

2 Magst du Computerspiele?

____.

3 Spielen Tom und Bob Fußball oder Handball?

____.

4 Isst Adam Obst oder Süßigkeiten?

____.

5 Helfen die Kinder auch im Garten?

____.

6 Gehst du zu Fuß zur Schule?

____.

Weniger als 4 Punkte? Wenn ja, arbeite bitte Kapitel 8 C nochmals durch! max. 6

Super fast lane

Bilde jeweils zwei Sätze wie vorgegeben.

✔ = richtig ✘ = falsch

1 (children/go) *Do children go* to school on Sundays? ✔

No, *children don't go* to school on Sundays. ✔

2 (the sun/shine) ______________________ at night?

No, ______________________ at night.

3 (cats/bark) ______________________ ?

No, ______________________ .

4 (Mrs Nunn/drive) ______________________ a taxi?

No, she ______________________ a taxi.

5 (Harry Potter/like) ______________________ his aunt and uncle?

No, he ______________________ his aunt and uncle.

6 (Kermit/love) ______________________ Miss Piggy?

No, he ______________________ Miss Piggy.

7 (elephants/walk) ______________________ on two legs?

No, they ______________________ on two legs.

8 (Captain Blaubär/tell) ______________________ true *(wahr)* stories?

No, he ______________________ true stories.

Weniger als 10 Punkte? Wenn ja, arbeite bitte Kapitel 8 A bis 8 C nochmals durch!

max 14

D *Do* als Hilfsverb: die verneinte Befehlsform

❶ **Don't be** so silly, Tom.
❷ **Don't make** such a noise, children.

▶ Die verneinte Befehlsform wird mit *do not/don't* + Infinitiv des Vollverbs gebildet, und zwar im Singular und im Plural ❶ ❷.

Exercise 4

Die Schilder, die du hier siehst, sind Verbotsschilder. Bilde Sätze mit *don't*, um jemandem zu sagen, was die Schilder bedeuten.

1 (cross) Don't cross the road.

2 (feed) ____________ the animals.

3 (swim) ____________ in the river.

4 (throw) ____________ bottles out of the window.

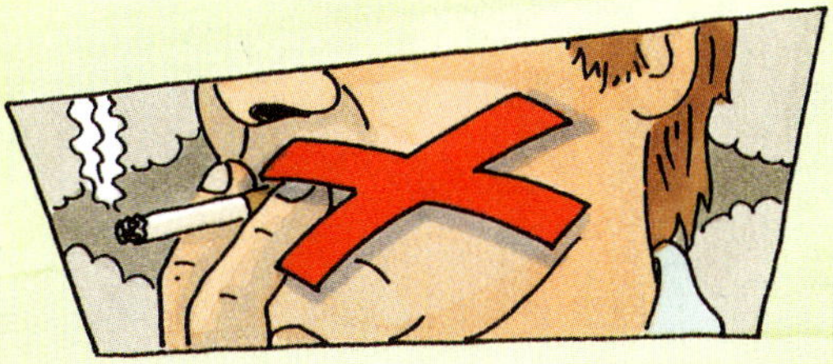

5 (smoke) ____________ on the train.

6 (play) ____________ radios on the beach.

7 (play) ____________ football in the car park.

8 (pick) ____________ flowers.

E *Do* als Vollverb und Hilfsverb

	Hilfsverb	Subjekt	Hilfsverb	Vollverb	andere Satzteile
❶		I	**don't**	**do**	sports.
❷	**Does**	Amy		**do**	the housework?
❸		You	**don't**	**do**	a test every day.
❹	**Do**	we		**do**	silly things sometimes?

- ▶ Lass dich nicht verwirren. In diesen Sätzen steht *do* zweimal, einmal als Vollverb und einmal als Hilfsverb.
- ▶ Wie die Sätze oben zeigen, bleibt das Vollverb *do* im Infinitiv stehen. Nur das Hilfsverb *do* ändert sich für die 3. Person Singular ❷.

Exercise 5

In dieser Übung sollst *du* die Fragen stellen.
Schreibe die passenden Kurzantworten dazu.

1 Amy does the housework every day.

Does Amy do the housework every day?

No, *she doesn't*.

2 Tom does the housework sometimes.

____________________ the housework sometimes?

Yes, ____________.

3 German children do their homework after school.

____________________ their homework after school?

Yes, ____________.

4 Bob and Tom do sports every day.

____________________ sports every day?

No, ____________.

5 Mr Carter sometimes does magic tricks.

____________________ magic tricks?

No, ____________________ .

6 Tom and Amy do their English homework together.

____

Yes, ____________________ .

Super fast lane

Bilde Sätze mit *do*. Achte auf das Satzzeichen am Ende des Satzes.

✔ = richtig ✘ = falsch

1 (Mrs Nunn/the housework)

Mrs Nunn does the housework in the evenings. ✔

2 (Tom/sport)

____ every Saturday?

3 (Bob/his homework)

____ every afternoon?

4 (Kirsty/a test)

____ every month?

5 (Miss Jones/not/the housework)

____ every day.

6 (Amy/not/her homework)

____ on the bus.

7 (Spooky/tricks)

____ tricks?

8 (Harry Potter/magic tricks)

____ magic tricks sometimes.

9 (Adam/not/homework)

____ at the weekends.

Weniger als 6 Punkte? Wenn ja, arbeite bitte Kapitel 8 A bis 8C und 8 E nochmals durch! max. 8

Family Tree

Sieh dir den Stammbaum genau an. Vervollständige dann die Sätze mit einem Wort aus der Liste.

mother daughter son uncle father
cousin grandfather grandchildren aunt

1 Alice is Andrew's ______________________________.

2 George is David's ______________________________.

3 Catherine is Tom and Sarah's ______________________________.

4 Tom is Alice's ______________________________.

5 Julia is Sarah's ______________________________.

6 Ray is Alice and David's ______________________________.

7 Tom and Sarah are Heather's ______________________________.

8 David is Julia's ______________________________.

9 Andrew is Alice and David's ______________________________.

10 Heather is Alice's ______________________________.

What are they going to be?

Was möchten diese Kinder werden, wenn sie älter sind?
Leider hat der Computer hier verrückt gespielt.
Kannst du die Berufe trotzdem erkennen?

1 Tom S C I D K E Y C O J

2 Adam A I R O L S

3 Kirsty C R A N D E

4 Dirk and Colin N A S C H I C E M

5 Jane X A T I R I D R E V

6 Peter S T R A N O T A U

7 Amy and Sue E C R E T A H S

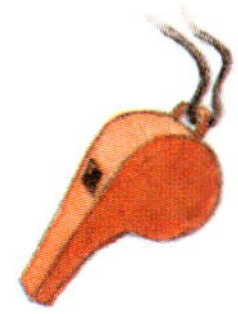

8 Bob A L L B O T O F P E Y L A R

9 Ann R E M A R F

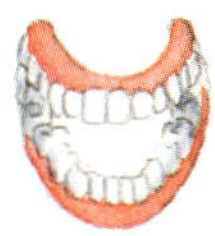

10 John S T I N D E T

1 Tom is going to be a *disc jockey* ______________.

2 Adam is going to be a *s* ______________.

3 Kirsty is going to be a *d* ______________.

4 Dirk and Colin are going to be *m* ______________.

5 Jane ______________ a *t* ______________.

6 Peter ______________ an *a* ______________.

7 Amy and Sue ______________ *t* ______________.

8 Bob ______________ *f* ______________.

9 Ann ______________ *f* ______________.

10 John ______________ *d* ______________.

9 Das *simple present*

A Form

B Gebrauch

C Die Verneinung

D Fragen

A Form

❶ Every year Amy's friends **come** to her birthday party.
❷ Kirsty sometimes **brings** a cake.
❸ Bob often **dances** with Amy at her party.
❹ Tom and Adam always **play** cards at parties.

▷ In Aussagesätzen hat das *simple present* folgende Formen:

I, you	play	go
he, she, it	play**s**	go**es**
we, you, they	play	go

▶ Ganz einfach ist es mit dem Anhängen von *-s* bei der 3. Person nicht. Es gibt bestimmte Schreibregeln, die du beachten musst:

- Bei einem Zischlaut *(-sh, -ss, -ch, -x)* am Ende des Wortes wird *-es* angehängt:

wash	he wash**es**	watch	he watch**es**
miss	she miss**es**	mix	it mix**es**

- Das *-y* nach einem Konsonanten wird zum *-i*. Hinzu kommt *-es*:

try	he tr**ies**	fly	it fl**ies**

- Das *-y* nach einem Vokal bleibt. Hinzu kommt nur *-s*:

say	he say**s**	buy	she buy**s**

Exercise 1

Unterstreiche alle Verben, die im *simple present* stehen.

The Cobbs live in England. They have two children. The children go to school by bus every morning. Mr Cobb works in Kingston. He always drives to work. At the weekend the children often play cricket with their friends and their dog, Spooky. Their friends often come from Germany and stay for two weeks. They always bring salami and marzipan. Mrs Cobb likes German salami very much.

Exercise 2

Schreibe die Form der folgenden Verben im *simple present* auf.

like/he	he likes	finish/he	________
carry/she	________	swim/she	________
cut/it	________	teach/they	________
guess/she	________	wash/I	________
find/he	________	eat/she	________
fly/it	________	go/he	________

B Gebrauch

❶ In Germany, most people **speak** German.
❷ He sometimes **surfs** the Internet.
❸ She often **meets** him.

▶ Wir benutzen das *simple present* für unveränderbare Tatsachen ❶ und um zu sagen, was man manchmal, oft, immer usw. macht ❷ ❸. Deshalb werden folgende Zeitadverbien sehr häufig mit dem *simple present* verwendet. Sie alle drücken eine Regelmäßigkeit aus und gelten deshalb als Signalwörter für das *simple present*:

- always, never,
- often, sometimes, now and then,
- usually, normally, regularly,
- every day, every week, every …
- on Mondays/…, at weekends/Christmas/…

Exercise 3

Suche für jeden Satz ein passendes Verb aus der Liste aus.
Du musst die Endung des Verbs aber – je nach Person – ändern und auch die Rechtschreibung beachten.

finish – get up – go – have – meet – ring – talk –
tidy up – walk – wash – watch – work – write

Every Monday it's the same story. Bob ________________ at 7 o'clock. He ________________ breakfast. Then he ________________ to school. His dad ________________ in the same *(im gleichen)* part of town. But he ________________ by bike. Bob's mother ________________ and ________________ the clothes. She ________________ her work in the afternoon. Sometimes she ________________ her friends and ________________ for hours! After school Bob ________________ his friends. In the evening his dad ________________ TV and his mother ________________ e-mails to her friends.

Fast lane

Schreibe mit den Satzteilen in der Tabelle acht vollständige Sätze über die Aktivitäten von Bob, Amy und Kirsty.

✔ = richtig ✘ = falsch

	Bob	Amy and Kirsty
every morning	get up at 7 o'clock	make breakfast
always	come home from school at 4 o'clock	go to school by bus
on Saturdays	buy a comic	play basketball
often	listen to CDs	meet their friends
never	walk to school	do the cooking

1 *Bob gets up at 7 o'clock every morning.* ✔

2 *He* ____________________________

3 *He* ____________________________

4 *He* ____________________________

5 *He* ____________________________

6 *Amy and Kirsty make breakfast every morning.* ✔

7 *They* ____________________________

8 *They* ____________________________

9 *They* ____________________________

10 *They* ____________________________

Weniger als 6 Punkte? Wenn ja, arbeite bitte Kapitel 9 A und 9 B nochmals durch!

max. 8

C Die Verneinung

❶ Kirsty **can't** speak German.
❷ Adam loves sweets, but **doesn't like** marzipan.
❸ We **don't like** hamburgers and chips much.

▶ Wenn es schon ein Hilfsverb im Satz gibt, müssen wir nur das Wörtchen *not/n't* unmittelbar dahinter setzen ❶.

▶ Wenn aber kein Hilfsverb vorhanden ist, müssen wir eine Form des Hilfsverbs *do* verwenden *(don't/doesn't)* ❷ ❸.

Exercise 4

Ergänze die Sätze mit Hilfe der Bilder durch eine Verneinung.

1 Tom plays football but he

doesn't play basketball.

2 A baker sells bread but he

____

3 My cat drinks milk but she

____

4 The boys have skateboards but they

__________ kickboards.

5 I speak English but I

____

6 Jim loves Janet but Janet

____

7 Cats sleep during the day but they

____

____

8 My mother makes cakes but she

____

D Fragen

	Hilfsverb	Subjekt	Adverb	Vollverb	Objekt	andere Satzteile
❶	**Can**	you		swim?		
❷	**Must**	we		go		to school on Saturday?
❸	**Do**	you	often	watch	TV?	
❹	**Does**	Spooky	always	bark		at the postman?

▶ Wenn kein anderes Hilfsverb wie *can* oder *must* passt, müssen wir *do/does* verwenden, um Fragen zu bilden.

Exercise 5

Forme die Aussagesätze in Fragen um.

1 Spooky likes cats.

Does Spooky like cats? ______________________

2 Mr Carter comes from Liverpool.

______________________ *from Liverpool?*

3 We live in a big house.

__________ *you* __________ in a big house?

4 The boys always run across the road.

______________________ across the road?

5 Kirsty has a new hairstyle.

______________________ a new hairstyle?

6 Bob can send e-mails to people all over the world.

______________________ e-mails to people all over the world?

7 Bob often sends a postcard to his friend in Canada.

______________________ to his friend in Canada?

Super fast lane

Bilde Sätze mit den vorgegebenen Satzteilen.
Beachte dabei die Symbole am Anfang der Schreiblinien:

[+] = Aussagesatz, [–] = verneinter Satz, und [?] = Fragesatz.

✔ = richtig ✘ = falsch

1 Adam/always/tease *(ärgern)*/Tweets

[+] Adam always teases Tweets. ✔

2 my father/work/in London

[+] ______________________

3 he/never/listen/to dance music

[–] ______________________

4 fish/live/in water

[?] ______________________

5 Dirk's sister/sometimes/help/him with his homework

[?] ______________________

____

6 Colin/often/write/to his grandmother/in Canada

[+] ______________________

____

7 we/watch/a lot of TV/at the weekend

[–] ______________________

____

8 the supermarket/sell/English books

[–] ______________________

____

9 dogs/sleep/at night

[?] ______________________

Weniger als 6 Punkte? Wenn ja, arbeite bitte Kapitel 9 A bis 9 D nochmals durch!

max. 8

10 Das *present progressive*

A Form

B Gebrauch

C Die Verneinung

D Fragen

E *Simple present* und *present progressive*

A Form

❶ – Amy, where's Spooky? – He **is playing** in the garden.
❷ Quick! The bus **is stopping**. We get out here.
❸ I**'m making** my bed and **putting** my jeans away.

▷ Wir bilden Aussagesätze im *present progressive* wie folgt:

	Langform	Kurzform
I	**am** play**ing**	'm play**ing**
you	**are** play**ing**	're play**ing**
he/she/it	**is** play**ing**	's play**ing**
we/you/they	**are** play**ing**	're play**ing**

▶ Wenn du Verben im *present progressive* schreibst, musst du die folgenden Schreibregeln beachten:

- bei Verben, die auf *-e* enden, wird bei der Bildung der *-ing*-Form der Endbuchstabe *-e* weggelassen:
  mak**e** – making
- bei Verben, die mit einem kurzen Vokal + folgendem Konsonanten – wie *-m, -n, -p,* oder *-t* – enden, wird der Konsonant verdoppelt:
  sto**p** – sto**pp**ing   pu**t** – pu**tt**ing

Exercise 1

Hier sollst du die vollständige Form des *present progressive* der angegebenen Verben in die Sätze einsetzen.

1 Tom _is doing_ (do) his homework at the moment,

and Amy ____________________ (help) her dad in the garden.

They ____________________ (cut) the grass.

2 Tom and Amy __________________ (tidy) their rooms. Tom ______________

(put) his clothes and books away, and Amy ______________ (make) her bed.

3 – Kirsty, where are you? – I ____________________ (watch) TV, Mum.

4 Hello, fans! I ___________________ (have) a great time on holiday in Spain.

I ______________ (write) this on the beach. Amy ________________ (swim)

in the sea, and of course Spooky _______________ (try) to run after her.

He ____________________ (bark) at her. And my parents?

They ____________________ (sleep) again.

B Gebrauch

❶ Tom and Amy **are helping** their father **at the moment**.
❷ I can't help you **now**, Tom. **I'm washing** my hair.
❸ Look what Spooky **is doing**!

- Wir benutzen das *present progressive*, um eine Handlung zu beschreiben, die zur Zeit des Sprechens oder Schreibens gerade geschieht, also im Gange ist.
- Im Deutschen gibt es die Verlaufsform des Verbs nicht. Wir verwenden stattdessen die Adverbien „im Moment", „jetzt" oder „gerade":

  Ich kann nicht kommen. Ich **wasche** mir **gerade** die Haare.
  I can't come. **I'm washing** my hair.

- Das *present progressive* wird häufig mit den Signalwörtern *now, at the moment* und *at present* benutzt.

Exercise 2

Sieh dir die Bilder an und sage, was Amy, Tom usw. gerade machen.

1 Bob is scoring a goal.

(score/a goal)

2 Tweets

(sing/in her cage)

3 Mrs Nunn

(run/to the bus stop)

4 Amy and Bob

(practise/a new dance)

5 Mrs Cobb

(make/a bed)

6 Adam

(sleep/in bed)

Fast lane

Übersetze die Sätze ins Englische.

✔ = richtig ✘ = falsch

1 Ich spiele (gerade) mit meinem Hund.

____

2 Tom repariert (im Moment) sein Fahrrad.

____

3 Meine Eltern schlafen (gerade). Sei bitte ruhig!

____

4 Ich räume (gerade) mein Zimmer auf.

____

5 Wir helfen (gerade) unseren Eltern in der Küche.

____

Weniger als 3 Punkte? Wenn ja, arbeite bitte Kapitel 10 A und 10 B nochmals durch! max. 5

C Die Verneinung

❶ – I hope you**'re not watching** TV again, Kirsty.
– No, I'**m not watching** TV, Mum. I'm reading!

❷ Where's Spooky? I hope he**'s not/isn't playing** on the beds.

▶ Um die verneinte Form im *present progressive* zu bilden, fügen wir einfach *not* hinzu, und zwar direkt vor die *-ing*-Form.

▷

	Langform	Kurzform
I	am not playing	'm not playing
you	are not playing	're not playing
he/she/it	is not playing	's not/isn't playing
we/you/they	are not playing	're not playing

Exercise 3

Setze die Aussagesätze unten in die verneinte Form um.
Du kannst dabei die Langform von *be* benutzen.

1 Tom is playing with Spooky.

He is not playing with Tweets.

2 Amy and Kirsty are waiting at the bus stop.

They ______________________________ at the station.

3 Mr Clarke is cleaning his bike.

He ______________________________ car.

4 We are listening to Adam's new cassette.

We ______________________________ to his new CD.

5 I am making my bed.

I ______________________________ Tom's bed.

6 You are putting away your jeans.

You ____ T-shirt.

D Fragen

❶ What **are you doing**, Bob? **Are you making** your bed?
❷ **Is Spooky playing** in the garden?

▶ Um Fragen zu bilden, tauschen *am/is/are* und das Subjekt des Satzes den Platz:

Aussage: Spooky **is** playing in the garden.

Frage: **Is** Spooky playing in the garden?

Exercise 4

Setze die Aussagesätze unten in die Frageform um.

1 Tom is playing football.

Is Tom playing football?

2 You are helping dad in the garden.

____________________ dad in the garden?

3 Kirsty is wearing her new dress.

____________________ her new dress?

4 Miss Jones and Mr Carter are sitting in the café.

____________________ in the café?

5 I am playing basketball for Green Park School on Saturday.

____________________ basketball for the school on Saturday?

6 We are doing a German test.

____________________?

7 Adam is eating sweets again.

____________________?

Super fast lane

In dieser Aufgabe kommen alle drei Satzformen des *present progressive* gemischt vor. In die Fragesätze musst du auch manchmal ein Personalpronomen *(I, you, he, she ...)* mit einsetzen.

✔ = richtig ✘ = falsch

bark – cut – do – do – go – listen – make – play – practise – stand – talk – try

Kirsty What *are you doing* at the moment, Amy? ✔

Amy Well, I __________ in the hall. I __________ to you on the phone.

Kirsty Ha, ha. Very funny.

Amy OK. Well, I __________ my homework, of course.

__________ your homework, too?

Kirsty No, I __________ posters out of a magazine.

And what about Tom?

Amy Oh, Tom! He __________ to some CDs with Bob.

Kirsty What? __________ those new dances?

Amy I don't know. They __________ a terrible noise.

Poor mum __________ to sleep, but she can't. Oh dear,

and now Spooky __________ at the boys.

He thinks they __________ with him.

Kirsty Oh, that's bad. __________ upstairs to stop him?

Amy Yes, bye, Kirsty.

Weniger als 8 Punkte? Wenn ja, arbeite bitte Kapitel 10 A bis 10 D nochmals durch! max 12

E *Simple present* und *present progressiv*

❶ – Come on, Tom, I **often** help you with your work. Now **I'm cutting** the grass and what are you doing? Nothing.

❷ – Yes, I am. **I'm sitting** in the sunshine **watching** you.

▶ Im Englischen – anders als im Deutschen – gibt es zwei Formen der Gegenwart. **Es ist nicht egal, welche Form benutzt wird:**

- Wir benutzen das *simple present*, um auszudrücken, dass etwas immer oder immer wieder, also sehr regelmäßig, passiert;
- wir benutzen das *present progressive*, um etwas zu beschreiben, das im Moment des Sprechens oder Schreibens vor sich geht.

Super fast lane

Setze die richtige Form der Gegenwart der angegebenen Verben in die Sätze ein.

✔ = richtig ✘ = falsch

1 – Look, Tom is winning (win) the race now. ✔

Bob ____________ (not run) very fast at the moment.

– That ____________ (be) funny because usually Bob ____________ (run) very fast.

I ____________ (think) he ____________ (not/try).

– You ____________ (be) right.

It ____________ (be) Tom's birthday today.

Bob ____________ (want) to give him a nice present.

2 – ____________ (you/tidy) your room, Kirsty, or ____________ (you/play) with my make-up again?

– I ____________ (tidy) my room, Mum, and I never ____________ (play) with make-up.

I ____________ (put) it on my face.

3 Kirsty and Amy ____________ (do) their homework.

But they ____________ (not/work) very hard.

Kirsty ____________ (think) maths is boring and Amy ____________ (hate) history.

Instead *(stattdessen)*, they ____________ (choose) a film they want to see later. Amy and Kirsty both ____________ (like) cartoons.

But first they ____________ (do) their exercises.

Weniger als 14 Punkte? Wenn ja, arbeite bitte Kapitel 9 und dieses Kapitel nochmals durch! max. 20

Vokabelübungen 4 • Tiere und Essen

The magic tree

Farmer Brown hat einen Baum, der viele Früchte und Gemüsesorten trägt. Sieh dir seinen Zauberbaum an und schreibe unten in Englisch auf, welche verschiedenen Obst- und Gemüsesorten – und wie viele von jeder Sorte – du gefunden hast.

Farmer Brown has got three apples, o__________,
s__________, b__________, p__________,
t__________, cabbage *(Kohl)* and
carrots *(Karotten)* on his magic tree.

Find that animal!

Ein Zootier ist weggelaufen. Hilf dem Tierwärter herauszufinden, welches es ist, indem du die Tierbilder den Wörtern zuordnest. Das Tier, das in der Liste steht, aber nicht abgebildet ist, ist das gesuchte Tier.

lion *tiger* *elephant* *monkey* *bear*

zebra *kangaroo* *tortoise* *penguin*

The missing animal is the ____.

11 Das *going to-future*

A Form

B Gebrauch

C Die Verneinung

D Fragen

A Form

❶ I **am going to have** a party next Friday.
❷ Kirsty **is going to buy** a new dress.
❸ We **are going to go** swimming later.

▷ Wir bilden das *going to-future* wie folgt:

Subjekt	*be*	*going to*	Infinitiv	andere Satzteile
I	am	going to	have	a party next Friday.
Kirsty	is	going to	buy	a new dress.
We	are	going to	go	swimming later.

B Gebrauch

▶ Wir benutzen das *going to-future*, wenn wir über etwas sprechen, das wir für die Zukunft fest planen oder vorhaben.

Exercise 1

Die Oak-Lane-Kinder und ihre Eltern und Lehrer planen ihr Wochenende.
Sage, was die Personen am Wochenende vorhaben.
Benutze das *going to-future*.

1 Mr Carter *is going to clean* ______ his bike.

2 Kirsty ______ in a disco.

3 Amy ______ basketball.

4 The Parkers ______ in the garden.

5 The Clarkes ______ their car.

6 Mrs Nunn ______ her bus.

C Die Verneinung

❶ I **am not going to stay** long.
❷ Adam **is not going to tell** Bob his secret *(Geheimnis)*.
❸ The children **are not going to spend** *(ausgeben)* their money on sweets.

!

▶ Um einen Satz mit dem *going to-future* zu verneinen, wird einfach das Wort *not* direkt hinter die Form von *to be (am/is/are)* eingefügt ❶ ❷ ❸.

Exercise 2

Schreibe die Sätze neu mit dem *going to-future*, sodass aus dem Wunsch eine Absicht wird.

1 Adam doesn't want to stay at home.

Adam *is not going to stay* at home.

2 Mr Carter doesn't want to move *(umziehen)*.

____

3 Amy doesn't want to watch the football match next Saturday.

____

4 Amy and Tom don't want to meet Mr Carter.

____

5 Mr and Mrs Parker don't want to go to a concert.

____

6 Kirsty doesn't want to see the new Walt Disney film.

____

D Fragen

1. **Are you going to leave** soon, Amy?
2. **Is Bob going to play** cards?
3. **Are they going to go** to the circus?

▶ Um Fragen zu bilden, tauschen *am/is/are* und das Subjekt des Satzes den Platz.

Aussage: **Bob is** going to play cards.

Frage: **Is Bob** going to play cards?

Exercise 3

Stelle Fragen wie vorgegeben.

1 My sister is going to go to the cinema later.

Is my sister going to go to the cinema later?

2 Bob is going to visit his grandparents this weekend.

______________________ his grandparents this weekend?

3 Amy is going to phone *(anrufen)* her friend Kirsty.

______________________?

4 Kirsty is going to play tennis with Tom.

______________________?

5 We are going to take the bus.

______________________?

6 Mrs Nunn is going to have a shower after work.

______________________?

Vokabelübungen 5 • Stadt und Verkehr

Worträtsel

Vervollständige das Puzzle mit Hilfe der Sätze unten. Wenn du alles richtig gemacht hast, ergibt sich von oben nach unten ein neues Wort.

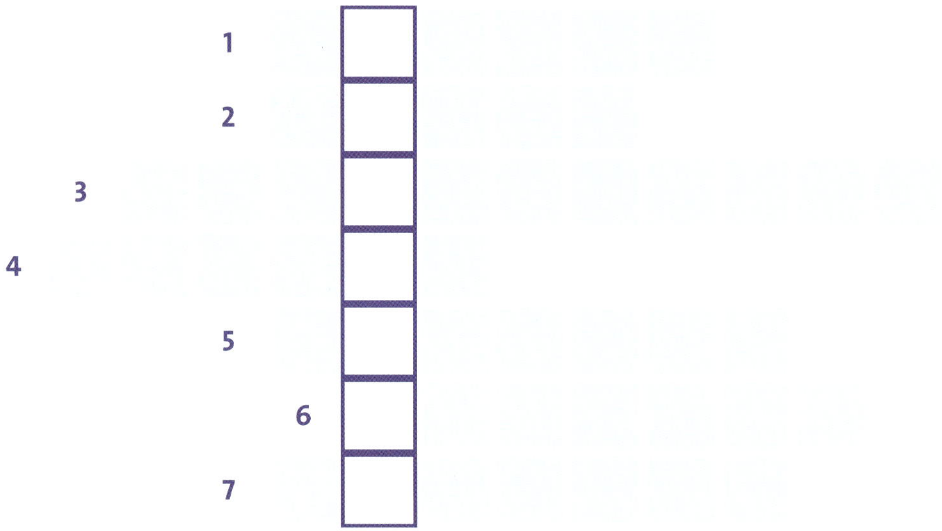

1 Children go here every day of the week.

2 In most towns in Britain the High Street is full of … .

3 People come here to buy groceries.

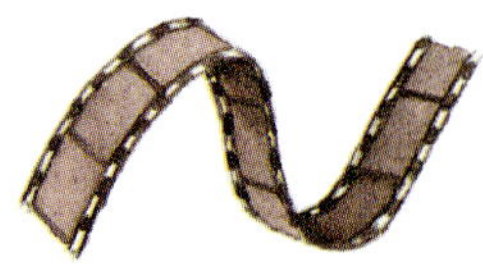

4 Lots of people like to go to this place to watch films.

5 You can come here to borrow books.

6 The train is leaving the … at 9 o'clock.

7 To watch a football match you go to the … .

Lösungswort: ____________________ .

Complete the sentences

Vervollständige die Sätze mit einem passenden Wort aus der unter jedem Satz stehenden Auswahl.

1 We have to be at the ____________ for 10 o'clock to catch the train.
A **park** **B** **station** **C** **car park**

2 We are going to play baseball in the ____________ this afternoon.
A **park** **B** **church** **C** **lake**

3 Tom and Amy are fishing in the ____________.
A **school** **B** **supermarket** **C** **harbour**

4 Mrs Cobb takes the number 72 ____________ to work.
A **bus** **B** **aeroplane** **C** **sportscar**

5 There are lots of small ____________ in England.
A **mountains** **B** **villages** **C** **people**

6 You can take your car from Germany to England on the ____________.
A **bus** **B** **ferry** **C** **motorway**

7 Mrs Cobb has a lot of money in the ____________.
A **baker's** **B** **bank** **C** **lake**

8 When you are sick you go to the ____________.
A **church** **B** **police station** **C** **hospital**

12 Die Wortstellung

A Aussagesatz und Nebensatz

	Subjekt	Verbteil	Objekt
❶	Kirsty	is	dancing.
❷	The boys and girls	are doing	their homework.
❸	Mr Parker	can speak	German.

▶ In Aussagesätzen lautet die Grundstellung immer **Subjekt – Verb – Objekt** (***S***traßen***v***erkehrs***o***rdnung/***SVO***).
Verb und Objekt gehören zusammen und es dürfen keine anderen Satzteile dazwischengestellt werden.

Exercise 1

Der Computer hat hier verrückt gespielt! Er hat die Sätze durcheinander gebracht. Bringe die Satzteile in die richtige Reihenfolge, indem du sie durch Ziffern kennzeichnest.

1 (3) baking cakes (2) is (1) Mrs Nunn
2 ◯ a lot of sweets ◯ eats ◯ Adam
3 ◯ is playing ◯ Spooky ◯ with Coco
4 ◯ Mr Clarke ◯ his new car ◯ is washing
5 ◯ is reading ◯ Miss Jones ◯ a book
6 ◯ Mr and Mrs Parker ◯ in the garden ◯ are working

! ▶ Auch für den englischen Nebensatz gilt: **Subjekt – Verb – Objekt**. Nebensätze fangen oft mit Wörtern wie *when*, *where* und *because* an.

▷

Hauptsatz				**Nebensatz**		
Subjekt	Verb	Objekt		Subjekt	Verb	Objekt
Adam	likes	Miss Jones	because	she	is	OK.

Exercise 2

Bringe zuerst die Wörter der Nebensätze in die richtige Reihenfolge. Verbinde dann die richtigen Haupt- und Nebensätze durch Linien zu einem sinnvollen Satz.

1 Mr Clarke works in the garden

when ◯ his shoes ◯ finds ◯ he.

2 Spooky sleeps on the sofa

when ②is ③nice ①the weather.

3 Mrs Cobb gets up early

because ◯ beats ◯ he always ◯ her.

4 Amy hates playing tennis with Tom

because ◯ so many sweets ◯ eats ◯ he.

5 Bob is going to play football

because ◯ the breakfast ◯ makes ◯ she.

6 Adam is never hungry

where ◯ is ◯ her homework.

7 Kirsty does not remember

when ◯ out ◯ the Cobbs are.

B Adverbien des Ortes und der Zeit

❶ Tom and Bob are camping **in the garden**.
❷ The bus leaves **at three o'clock**.
❸ Miss Jones arrives **at school at 8.45 every morning**.
❹ **Tomorrow** we are going to have a picnic.

- Mit Adverbien des Ortes wird ein Ort oder eine Richtung beschrieben. Mit Adverbien der Zeit wird ein Zeitpunkt oder ein Zeitraum beschrieben. Beide stehen normalerweise am Ende des Satzes ❶ ❷.
- Kommen eine Orts- und eine Zeitangabe gemeinsam im Satz vor, dann ist die Reihenfolge Ort vor Zeit ❸.
  Stehen in einem Satz zwei Orts- oder Zeitangaben, so gilt: die detailliertere Angabe steht vor der allgemeineren Angabe ❸.
- Wenn wir die Zeitangabe betonen wollen, kann sie auch am Anfang des Satzes stehen. Es ist wichtig, sich dabei zu merken, dass im Englischen – anders als im Deutschen – das Subjekt und das Verb nicht vertauscht werden ❹:

We play football on Saturdays.	On Saturdays **we play** football.
Wir spielen samstags Fußball.	Samstags **spielen wir** Fußball.

Exercise 3

Setze Ziffern ein, um die Orts- und Zeitangaben in die richtige Reihenfolge zu bringen.

1 The Cobb children go (2) in Kingston (1) to school
2 We are all going ◯ in London ◯ on Saturday ◯ to the cinema
3 Mr Nunn goes ◯ at 7 o'clock ◯ every day ◯ to work
4 The film is on ◯ at 8.30 ◯ at the youth club ◯ on Friday
5 Adam is going ◯ in Greece ◯ this summer ◯ to Athens
6 Miss Jones wants to move *(umziehen)* ◯ at the weekend ◯ in Penny Street ◯ into her new flat

C Adverbien der Häufigkeit

	Subjekt	Hilfsverb	Adverb	Verb	Objekt	Orts-/Zeitangabe
❶	The boys		**often**	play	football	on Saturdays.
❷	You	can	**usually**	buy	good CDs	at that shop.
❸	We		**sometimes**	visit	my uncle	in London.

▶ In der Regel stellen wir Häufigkeitsadverbien wie *often, usually* und *sometimes* unmittelbar vor das Vollverb.

Exercise 4

Setze das Häufigkeitsadverb in Klammern mit einem Pfeil an die richtige Stelle.

1 (sometimes) Tom ○ forgets ○ his maths homework ○.

2 (often) Amy and Kirsty ○ go ○ to the disco ○ on Fridays ○.

3 (never) Bob and Tom ○ meet ○ at the youth club ○ in Davis Street ○.

4 (usually) Mr Clarke ○ helps ○ Mrs Clarke ○ with the housework ○.

5 (always) Mrs Parker ○ is ○ working ○ in the garden ○.

6 (sometimes) Spooky ○ is ○ a naughty *(ungezogen)* little dog ○.

13 Fragewörter

A *How? what? when? where? which? who? whose? why?*

B *What?* und *who?* als Subjekt

A *How? what? when? where? which? who? whose? why?*

❶ **How** do they **get** to school?
❷ **Where are** Spooky and Coco?
❸ **When does** the train **arrive**?
❹ **Who can** I ask to my party?

- Bei Fragen, die mit Fragewörtern (*how?, what?* usw.) gebildet sind, steht dieses am Anfang des Fragesatzes.

Frage ohne Fragewort:	Can Bob come round today?
Frage mit Fragewort:	**When** can Bob come round today?

- Fragen mit Fragewörtern werden mit einer Form von *to be* oder mit einem Hilfsverb gebildet ❷ ❹.
- Wenn keine Form von *to be* und kein anderes Hilfsverb da sind, steht *do/does* nach dem Fragewort ❶ ❸.
- Die Satzstellung ist die gleiche wie bei Fragen ohne ein Fragewort. Vergleiche Seite 93.

Exercise 1

Bilde Fragen mit *how?*, *when?*, *where?*, *who?*, *why?*.
In den unterstrichenen Satzteilen steht, wonach du fragen sollst.

1 Tom and Amy Cobb live in Oak Lane, Kingston.

Where do Tom and Amy Cobb live? ______

2 Tom plays football every Saturday.

Who plays football every Saturday ______?

3 Kirsty gets up at 7 every morning.

______?

4 I like Miss Jones because she's nice.

______ you ______?

5 I'm going to see Kirsty at the youth club disco.

______ you ______?

6 The post office is in Briany Road next to the pub.

______?

7 Look, Amy, you do the exercise like this.

______ I ______?

8 My birthday is in May.

______ your ______?

9 Adam feels good.

______?

10 Bob is wearing shorts because it's hot.

______?

- Man verwendet *what?* meistens, wenn man aus einer unbegrenzten Anzahl von Dingen wählen kann.
- *Which?* verwendet man meistens, wenn man die Wahl zwischen einer begrenzten Anzahl von Dingen hat.

What are your favourite colours?	*Was/Welches ...?*
Which colour would you like? Red or blue?	*Welche ...?*

Exercise 2

Frage nach den unterstrichenen Dingen.
Verwende die Fragewörter *what?* und *which?*

1 The book is on the table.

What is on the table ?

2 Kirsty likes the new Spielberg film.

Which film does Kirsty like ?

3 Amy gives Tweets water every morning.

______________________________ ?

4 Toffees are Adam's favourite sweets.

______________________________ ?

5 Bob likes the red jacket.

______________________________ ?

6 I want to buy the new magic dictionary.

______________ you ______________ ?

▶ Wir benutzen *whose?*, um zu fragen, wem etwas gehört.
Whose book is this? – (It's) Kirsty's.
Whose CDs are these? – (They're) Amy's.

Exercise 3

Sieh dir die Bilder an und stelle Fragen mit *whose*?

1 Whose dog is Spooky?
(dog)

2 ______________________________
______________________ Tweets?
(bird)

3 ______________________________
__________________ Miss Jones?
(form teacher)

4 ______________________________
____________________ Adam?
(neighbour)

5 ______________________________
__________________ on the desk?
(bag)

B *What?* und *who?* als Subjekt

	Objekt	Hilfsverb	Subjekt	Vollverb	andere Satzteile
❶	**What**	are	you	doing	in the garden, Adam?
❷	**Who**	do	you	play	cards with, Tom?
❸			**What**	happens	at the end of the book?
❹			**Who**	is coming	to your party, Kirsty?

- In den Sätzen ❶ und ❷ sind *what?* und *who?* Objekt des Satzes. Wir brauchen immer ein Hilfsverb, also *do, are* usw., um eine Frage zu bilden.
- In den Sätzen ❸ und ❹ sind *what?* und *who?* Subjekt des Satzes. In diesem Fall brauchen wir kein Hilfsverb, um eine Frage zu bilden.

Exercise 4

Bilde Fragen mit *what?, who?*.
in dieser Übung ist das Fragewort immer das Subjekt des Satzes.

1 Who __________ goes out with Bob every weekend? – Amy does.

2 __________ is making that noise? – Spooky is.

3 __________ often sings a lovely song? – Tweets does.

4 __________ makes you nervous? – Tests do.

5 __________ plays with Coco? – Spooky does.

6 __________ makes Mr Carter angry? – Noisy pupils.

Super fast lane

Bilde Fragen mit *how? what? when? where? which? who? whose? why?*.
In den unterstrichenen Satzteilen steht, wonach du fragen sollst.
Bei den Sätzen mit *who?* oder *what?* achte besonders darauf, ob es sich dabei um das Subjekt oder das Objekt des Satzes handelt.

✔ = richtig ✘ = falsch

1 We are having fish and chips for tea today.

What are we having for tea today ? ✔

2 Bob is happy because he has a new football.

______________________________?

3 Accidents happen every day.

______________________________?

4 I'm reading a book.

______________ *you* ______________?

5 Amy is going out with Kirsty today.

______________________________?

6 Amy loves Bob Parker.

______________________________?

7 We have lunch at 12 o'clock.

______________ *you* ______________?

8 Kirsty likes the red but not the green blouse.

______________________________?

9 Kirsty Nunn lives in Apple Road.

______________________________?

10 It is my computer game.

______________________________?

Weniger als 6 Punkte? Wenn ja, arbeite bitte Kapitel 13 A und 13 B nochmals durch! max. 9

14 Mengenangaben

A *Some, any* und *no* …

B *Much/many* und *a lot of/lots of*

A *Some, any* und *no* …

❶ I'd like **some** apples and **some** tea, please.
❷ Have you got **any** fresh tomatoes, please?
❸ No, I'm sorry. We **don't** have **any** tomatoes today. /
We have **no** tomatoes today.

▶ *Some* benutzen wir in bejahten Aussagesätzen ❶.

▶ *Any* benutzen wir bei „echten Fragen", wenn wir nicht wissen, wie die Antwort lauten wird ❷.
Wir benutzen *any* außerdem in verneinten Aussagesätzen ❸.

▶ *No* … können wir statt *not any* verwenden ❸.

Exercise 1

Sieh dir die Leute auf Seite 103 an. Jeder hat zwei Fäden, die zu einem Luftballon führen. Das lachende Gesicht in dem Ballon bedeutet, dass die Person die Sachen besitzt; ein trauriges Gesicht bedeutet, dass die Person die Sachen nicht besitzt. Schreibe auf, was du herausgefunden hast.

1 Mr Carter has got *some pens* ,
but he hasn't got *any paper* .

2 Miss Jones has got ______________________,
but she hasn't got ______________________.

3 Adam has got ______________________,
but he hasn't got ______________________.

4 Bob has got ______________________________,

but he hasn't got ______________________________.

5 Amy has got ______________________________,

but she hasn't got ______________________________.

6 Kirsty has got ______________________________,

but she hasn't got ______________________________.

7 Tom has got ______________________________,

but he hasn't got ______________________________.

B *Much/many* und *a lot of/lots of*

❶ How **much** tea have we got?
– Not **much**. Let's buy some?

❷ How **many** CDs has Adam got?
– Not **many**. Six, I think.

❸ Adam gets **a lot of** pocket-money, and buys **lots of** sweets with it.

- *Much* und *many* werden meist in verneinten Aussagesätzen und in Fragesätzen verwendet ❶ ❷.
- In bejahten Aussagesätzen ist *a lot of/lots of* gebräuchlicher ❸.

▷	+	−	?
zählbar	a lot of lots of	(not) many	many
nicht zählbar	a lot of lots of	(not) much	much

Exercise 2

Unterstreiche die Wörter, die nicht zählbar sind.

apple – bag – book – bread – butter – child – coffee – exercise *(Aufgabe)* – girl – homework – horse – lemonade – love – meat – milk – money – newspaper – potato – sugar – time *(Zeit)* – tea – toy – training – water – work

Exercise 3

Setze *much*, *many* oder *a lot of* in die Sätze ein.

1 Adam spends ________________ money on sweets.

2 Do you know ________________ people in Germany?

3 We don't have ________________ time. Hurry up!

4 Bob hasn't got ________________ money with him,

but he's got quite ______________ money in his piggy bank *(Spardose)*.

5 How ______________ bottles of lemonade do we have?

6 ______________ boys play football in school.

Super fast lane

Setze *some, any, much, many* oder *a lot of* in den Dialog ein.

✔ = richtig ✘ = falsch

Mrs C Do you need ___________ food from the supermarket?

Mrs P Yes, can you buy me ___________ sugar, please?

Mrs C Of course. How ___________ sugar do you want?

Mrs P Just one kilo, please. Oh, and we haven't got ___________ eggs.
Please, bring me ___________ eggs, too.

Mrs C OK. How ___________ do you want?

Mrs P Ten. Oh, and I need ________ cheese. Bring ________________ cheese,
please, because I want to make ___________ cheese salad tonight.

Mrs C Yes, all right. ___________ cheese, too, then. What about butter?
Do you need ___________ butter?

Mrs P Yes, of course. Thank you. I haven't got ____________________ butter.

Mrs C What a surprise! How ___________ do you need?

Mrs P Half a pound, please. Oh, and ___________ bananas, I ...

Mrs C Look, this is quite ___________ of shopping.
Why don't you come with me?

Mrs P I haven't got _________________ time, dear. I have such ___________
things to do, and I haven't got ___________ help at all.

Weniger als 13 Punkte? Wenn ja, arbeite bitte Kapitel 14 A und 14 B nochmals durch. max. 18

15 Präpositionen

A Präpositionen des Ortes

B Präpositionen der Bewegung

C Präpositionen der Zeit

A Präpositionen des Ortes

1. Spooky is **in** the kitchen.
2. He is **under** the table.
3. Now he is **on** the table.
4. Now he is **at** the window.

! ▶ In den Sätzen oben sagen uns die Präpositionen, **wo** Spooky ist. Sie sind also **Präpositionen des Ortes**.

▷ Hier ist eine Übersicht der Ortspräpositionen:

at	*an*	next to	*neben*
behind	*hinter*	on	*auf*
between	*zwischen*	outside	*draußen*
in front of	*vor*	under	*unter*
inside	*in*		

Exercise 1

Ordne jedem Bild die richtige der oben aufgelisteten Präpositionen zu.

1 *in front of* ____________

2 ____________

3 ____________

4 ____________

5 ____________

6 ____________

7 ____________

8 ____________

9 ____________

Exercise 2

Beschreibe, wo die Kinder in Miss Jones' Klasse sitzen.
Hier sind ihre Schreibtische mit Namenskarten.

1 Amy sits *next to* Kirsty.

2 Adam sits ______________ Bob and Dirk.

3 Bob sits ______________ Susan.

4 Mike sits ______________ Adam.

5 Mike sits ______________ John and Susan.

6 Dirk sits ______________ John.

7 Tom sits ______________ Kirsty.

8 Jane sits ______________ Amy.

9 Bob sits ______________ Adam and Jane.

10 Dirk sits ______________ Adam.

B Präpositionen der Bewegung

❶ Spooky is running **out of** the garden, and **along** the street.
❷ He is going **across** the street, and **into** the park.

▶ *Out of, along, across* und *into* drücken eine Bewegung aus.
Sie sind also **Präpositionen der Bewegung**.

▷ Hier ist eine Übersicht der Präpositionen der Bewegung:

across	*hinüber*	out of	*heraus*
after	*nach(her), hinter(her)*	over	*über*
against	*gegen*	past	*vorbei*
along	*entlang*	round	*um … herum*
down	*hinunter*	through	*hindurch*
from	*aus … heraus*	to	*zu, nach, in*
into	*in … hinein*	towards	*auf … zu*
off	*weg, davon*	under	*unter (hindurch)*
onto	*auf*	up	*nach oben, hinauf*

Exercise 3

Beschreibe den Weg des Flusses von seiner Quelle bis zum Meer.

The stream (*Bach*) comes __out of__ the ground. It runs __d________ the hill, __r________ some rocks, __t________ a forest (*Wald*), __o________ a path and __i________ a big river. The river goes ____________ a bridge (*Brücke*) and __p________ a little village and ____________ the sea.

C Präpositionen der Zeit

❶	**at** 4 o'clock/6.30/...	*Uhrzeit*
	at night	*nachts*
	at the weekend	*am Wochenende*
	at Christmas/Easter/...	*religiöse Feste*
❷	**on** Monday/Tuesday/...	*Wochentage*
	on March 14th/September 2nd/...	*Daten*
❸	**in** the morning/afternoon/evening	*Tageszeit*
	in May/June/...	*Monate*
	in spring/summer/...	*Jahreszeit*
	in 1066/1974/...	*Jahreszahl*

Exercise 4

Trage *in*, *at* oder *on* ein.

1 Adam often goes to bed late __________ night and gets up early __________ the morning.

2 He eats his breakfast __________ a few minutes during the week but __________ the weekend he has lots of time.

3 School starts again __________ 7th September.

4 He always goes to Spain __________ the summer but he stays __________ home __________ Christmas and __________ Easter.

5 It often snows __________ winter.

6 So Adam often goes ice skating __________ weekends __________ January.

7 He sometimes goes swimming with his friends __________ Saturdays __________ the summer.

David Clarke, Ingrid Preedy

Besser in Englisch

5. Klasse • Lösungsheft

Cornelsen
Power Learning

❶ Das Nomen

Exercise 1

1 (At school) chairs – classes – desks – felt tips – girls – lessons – pens – pencils – shelves – tables
2 (Clothes) blouses – coats – dresses – jackets – pullovers – shoes
3 (Food and drink) apples – biscuits – cakes – cheeses – drinks – oranges – potatoes – sandwiches – sausages – tomatoes
4 (Transport) bicycles – buses – cars – lorries – planes – ships – taxis – trains – vans – wheels

Exercise 2

two babies – two boxes – three buses – three children – two feet – two knives – four matches – three men – three toothbrushes – two women

Super fast lane

children – class – party – parties – boys – girls – knives – forks – cups – glasses – name – lists – food – biscuits – cake – sweets – boy – teeth

Exercise 3

2 Adam's sweets
3 Miss Jones' bag
4 Mr Clarke's car
5 the wheel of the bike (bicycle)
6 Bob and Tom's football
7 Tweet's cage
8 Mrs Nunn's bus

Fast lane

1 my parents' garden
2 Amy's dog – Mrs Cobb's bird
3 the window of Bob's room
4 Adam's house – end of the street
5 Tom's maths book – six pages of the book
6 The colour of his eyes
7 The sleeves of Kirsty's dress

Vokabelübungen 1

Länder und Reisen

1 Hidden Countries

A	D	R	P	L	E	R	Z	T	I	U	S
P	O	R	T	U	G	A	L	S	S	E	C
F	A	L	F	A	T	L	A	P	L	I	O
A	U	S	T	R	A	L	I	A	I	A	T
M	E	N	G	E	A	J	N	I	R	B	L
E	E	N	G	L	A	N	D	N	E	U	A
R	Q	H	L	E	S	I	C	D	L	I	N
I	E	S	A	N	R	K	L	E	A	N	D
C	I	E	L	J	D	M	N	C	N	J	L
A	U	S	T	R	I	A	A	A	D	S	E
R	E	G	T	O	P	B	A	N	A	L	A
E	U	W	E	A	D	E	F	H	Y	K	T

1 Portugal
2 Australia
3 England
4 Austria
5 America
6 Spain
7 Ireland
8 Scotland
9 France
10 Germany

2 Holiday

1 holiday
2 train
3 postcards
4 breakfast
5 plane
6 campsite
7 sunglasses
8 beach
9 journey
10 mountains

❷ Die Pronomen

Exercise 1

2 she
3 she
4 it
5 they
6 she
7 they

Exercise 2

2 him
3 them
4 them
5 it
6 her
7 them

Fast lane

They – them – They – her – they – they – him – them – him – they – They – it – she – it – She – he – it – I – you – me – he – You – me – I – You – I – them

Exercise 3

her – Her – Your – their – their – his – their – her – my – my

Fast lane

1 for his birthday – His sister
2 her bus
3 his sweets – his desk – his English book
4 its wing
5 their school bags – their back
6 her bag

Exercise 4

2 that
3 this
4 those
5 these
6 that
7 this
8 those

Fast lane

2 that – that – that
3 these – those
4 These
5 this – That – this – That – this – this – that – This

Vokabelübungen 2

1 Crazy, Crazy

(cake), cakes – candle, candles – camera, cameras – car, cars – card, cards – cat, cats – chair, chairs – cheese, cheese – child, children – clock, clocks – coat, coats – comic, comics – cloud, clouds – cow, cows – cup, cups

2 Hidden sentence

On the way to the park Spooky sees a cat and runs after it.

❸ Der Artikel

Exercise 1

(the airport) – the aunt – the egg – the English book – the exercise – the ice cream – the invitation – the old town – the uncle

Exercise 2

1 Kirsty doesn't live in Oak lane. She lives in (the) white house at the end of Cherry Tree Road.
2 Most of the boys at Green Park School like football, but a lot of the girls think that basketball or volleyball is more fun.
3 – Do you go to school by bus or by train?
– Well, I go by taxi. The taxi belongs to my dad, you see.
4 – Should we go to town today? The film about the Eskimos is on at the cinema in Station road.
Yes, OK. We can go by bike.

Exercise 3

(a) man – (an) old book – an accident – an address – a bag – a cake – a DVD player – a dirty shoe – an egg – an English book – an expensive T-shirt – a family – a flat – a guitar – a hand – a hotel – an hour – an idea – a CD – a magazine – a mistake – a noise – an old car – an orange – a pen – pet – question – an uncle – an underground train – a uniform – an untidy room – a village – a wall – a year – a yellow apple – a zoo

Fast lane

1 a bus driver
2 has (got) a headache – has (got) a cold
3 in a hurry/in a rush
4 ride a bike
5 a long time
6 has (got) a uniform
7 (a) quarter to eight
8 What a shame!
9 is showering/is having a shower
10 wants to be a teacher/wants to become a teacher

❹ Zahlen

Exercise 1

fourteen – eighty-nine – eleven – fifty-two – fifteen – thirty-three – nineteen – ninety-eight – twelve – forty-five – two hundred and fifteen

Exercise 2

one radio – nineteen sweets – thirteen books – four CDs – eight pens – three posters – eleven toy cars – one CD player

Exercise 3

2 (six –) nine – O – six – three – one
3 Manchester one, Liverpool nil/nothing
4 two thousand and eight
5 nineteen ninety-six
6 one thousand three hundred and eighty-six

Fast lane

2 eighty-one
3 thirty-one
4 one hundred
5 twelve
6 eight
7 one thousand
8 fifty
9 forty-one (forty-two)

Exercise 4

1 (T)
2 H
3 I
4 S
5 I
6 S
7 E
8 A
9 S
10 Y

Dein Satz: This is easy.

Fast lane

2 fourteenth
3 seventh
4 twelfth
5 ninth
6 nineteenth
7 third
8 eighth
9 twenty-third
10 fifteenth
11 eighteenth
12 twentieth

❺ Uhrzeiten und Datum

Exercise 1

Exercise 2

2 twenty-five (minutes) past eight/ eight twenty-five
3 twenty-five (minutes) to ten/nine thirty-five
4 five (minutes) to nine/eight fifty-five
5 half (past) four/four thirty
6 (a) quarter to two/one forty-five
7 twenty (minutes) to four/three forty
8 (a) quarter past eleven/eleven fifteen

Fast lane

2 five (minutes) past eight
3 nine o'clock
4 (a) quarter to eleven/ten forty-five
5 (a) quarter to three/two forty five
6 half (past) four/four thirty
7 twenty-two (minutes) past five/ five twenty-two

Exercise 3

2 April the first/the first of April
3 August the twenty-third/ the twenty-third of August
4 January the thirty-first/ the thirty-first of January
5 December the twentieth/ the twentieth of December
6 November the third/ the third of November

Exercise 4

2 on 13th May
3 on 7th September
4 on 2nd October
5 on 1st February
6 on 29th May

Fast lane

2 the twenty-first of March
3 on the tenth of April
4 is on the sixteenth of May

5 is on the twelfth of July
6 is on the fourth of August
7 is ('s) on the eighth of September
on the (*freie Lösung*)

❻ Das Verb be – Gegenwart

Exercise 1

(is) – am – is – are – are – am – is – is – am – is – is

Exercise 2

2 are not/aren't
3 is not/isn't
4 are not/aren't
5 is not/isn't
6 I am/I'm not

Fast lane

2 is not/isn't
3 are not/aren't
4 is not/isn't
5 are not/aren't
6 is not/isn't
7 are not/aren't
8 is not/isn't

Exercise 3

2 Is Bob Amy's brother?
3 Is Tom the captain this year?
4 Are Amy and Bob good friends?
5 Is Amy Kirsty's best friend?
6 Are you in the team for the next match?

Fast lane

2 Are the Cobb children
3 Is Old Carter
4 Is Spooky
5 Am I
6 Are Hamburg and Cologne
7 Is Mrs Nunn
8 Is Amy

Super fast lane

2 Is Tom Kirsty's brother?
– Tom isn't Kirsty's brother.
3 Is London a small town?
– London isn't a small town.
4 Is Miss Jones Mr Carter's friend?
– Miss Jones isn't Mr Carter's friend.
5 Is Mr Carter a good teacher?
– Mr Carter isn't a good teacher.
6 Is Kirsty Tom's girlfriend?
– Kirsty isn't Tom's girlfriend.
7 Is Harry Potter's aunt nice?
– Harry Potter's aunt isn't nice.
8 Is Green Park a bad school?
– Green Park isn't a bad school.

Exercise 4

2 Don't be – be helpful
3 Don't be – be good
4 Don't be so silly – be sensible
5 Don't be so careless – be more careful

Exercise 5

It's Saturday, and Tom and Amy are waiting for their friends. They're having a party. "Where's the coke?" asks Amy. "Tom, there's no coke." "Yes, there is," says Tom. "Twelve bottles. They're in the kitchen. That's enough. I always buy it at Smith's. You know, the shop in Queen's Street. Coke's cheap there." "Oh," says Amy, "you're just like dad. He's always looking for cheap things, too." "What's wrong with that?" says Tom. "We're not rich!"

Fast lane

He's – I'm – Old Carter's – You're – that's – You're – you're – I'm – he's – Amy's – You're not/you aren't – you're not/you aren't

❼ Das Verb have – Gegenwart

Exercise 1

(has) – has – has – has – have – has – have

Exercise 2

2 do not/don't have
3 does not/doesn't have
4 does not/doesn't have
5 do not/don't have
6 do not/don't have
7 do not/don't have

Fast lane

does not (doesn't) have – does not (doesn't) have – do not (don't) have – do not (don't) have – do not (don't) have – do not (don't) have – do not (don't) have – do not (don't) have

Exercise 3

3 Does Tom Cobb have
4 Does Kirsty have
5 Does Amy have
6 Do Tom and Bob have a shower
7 Does Adam have
8 Do I have

Fast lane

Do you have – have – Do you have (any) – Do you have – have – Do we have/Do you have – have – Do you have – have

Super fast lane

1 Spooky does not (doesn't) have a bath
2 Do you have time?
3 Bob has a good idea
4 Does Mr Clarke have breakfast
5 Does Bob have
6 Amy does not (doesn't) have (any)
7 Mrs Nunn does not (doesn't) have a
8 Does Adam have
9 I do not (don't) have
10 Do Mr and Mrs Clarke have

Exercise 4

(have got) – have got – has – have – has – has – have got – has – has – has – has got – have got – have got – have

Exercise 5

2 has not/hasn't got
3 have not/haven't got
4 I have not/haven't got a felt tip.
5 Adam has not/hasn't got a new cap.
6 The Parkers have not/haven't got a swimming pool.
7 Kirsty has not/hasn't got a camcorder.

Exercise 6

2 Has Bob got a football?
3 Has Kirsty got a CD player?
4 Has Adam got a blue cap?
5 Have Mr and Mrs Clarke got a car?
6 Has Amy got a kickboard?

❽ Das Verb do – Gegenwart

Exercise 1

1 does
2 does
3 do
4 does
5 do
6 do

Exercise 2

2 does not (doesn't) work – works
3 does not (doesn't) drive – drives
4 does not (don't) live – live
5 does not (doesn't) eat – eats
6 does not (doesn't) go to the cinema with Miss Jones. Mrs Clarke goes to the cinema with Mrs Carter.
7 do not (don't) watch videos at the weekend. The children play games at the weekend.

Fast lane

1 Tom and Bob do not (don't) play
2 children do not (don't) go
3 Amy and Tom do not (don't) live
4 I do not (don't) go
5 does not (doesn't) play
6 you do not (don't) do

Exercise 3

2 Do the children live – do
3 Does Adam like – doesn't
4 Does Adam eat – does
5 Do Tom and Amy go – they don't
6 Does Kirsty help her mother a lot? – she does
7 Does Mr Cater walk to school? – he doesn't
8 Does Green Park win every football match? – it doesn't

Fast lane

1 Does Kirsty live
2 Do you like
3 Do Tom and Bob play
4 Does Adam eat
5 Do the children help
6 Do you walk

Super fast lane

2 Does the sun shine – the sun doesn't (does not) shine
3 Do cats bark? – cats don't (do not) bark
4 Does Mrs Nunn drive – doesn't (does not)
5 Does Harry Potter like – doesn't (does not) like
6 Does Kermit love – doesn't (does not) love
7 Do elephants walk – don't (do not) walk
8 Does Captain Blaubär tell – doesn't (does not) tell

Exercise 4

2 Don't feed
3 Don't swim
4 Don't throw
5 Don't smoke
6 Don't play
7 Don't play
8 Don't pick

Exercise 5

2 Does Tom do – he does
3 Do German children do – they do
4 Do Bob and Tom do – they don't
5 Does Mr Carter sometimes do – he doesn't
6 Do Tom and Amy do their English homework together? – they do

Super fast lane

2 Does Tom do sport
3 Does Bob do his homework
4 Does Kirsty do
5 Miss Jones doesn't (does not) do
6 Amy doesn't (does not) do her homework
7 Does Spooky do
8 Harry Potter does
9 Adam doesn't (does not) do his homework

Vokabelübungen 3

1 Family tree

1 daughter
2 uncle
3 mother
4 cousin
5 aunt
6 grandfather
7 grandchildren
8 son
9 father
10 grandmother

2 What are they going to be?

1 disc jockey
2 sailor
3 dancer
4 mechanics
5 is going to be a taxi driver
6 is going to be an astronaut
7 are going to be teachers
8 is going to be a football player
9 is going to be a farmer
10 is going to be a dentist

❾ Das simple present

Exercise 1

the Cobbs live in England. They have two children. The children go to school by bus every morning. Mr Cobb works in Kingston. He always drives to work. At the weekend the children often play cricket with their friends and their dog, Spooky. Their friends often come from Germany and stay for two weeks. They always bring salami and marzipan. Mrs Cobb likes German salami very much.

Exercise 2

(he likes) – he finishes – she carries – she swims – it cuts – they teach – she guesses – I wash – he finds – she eats – it flies – he goes

Exercise 3

gets up – has – walks – works – goes – tidies up – washes – finishes – rings – talks – meets – watches – writes

Fast lane

2 always comes home from school at 4 o'clock.
3 buys a comic on Saturdays.
4 often listens to CDs.
5 never walks to school.
7 always go to school by bus.
8 play basketball on Saturdays.
9 often meet their friends.
10 never do the cooking.

Exercise 4

2 doesn't sell apples.
3 doesn't drink lemonade.
4 don't have kickboards.
5 don't speak French.
6 doesn't love Jim.
7 don't sleep during the night.
8 doesn't make bread.

Exercise 5

2 Does Mr Carter come from
3 Do you live
4 Do the boys always run
5 Does Kirsty have
6 Can Bob send
7 Does Bob often send a postcard

Super fast lane

2 My Father works in London.
3 He never listens to dance music.
4 Do fish live in water?
5 Does Dirk's sister sometimes help him with his homework?
6 Colin often writes to his grandmother in Canada.
7 We don't (do not) watch a lot of TV at the weekend.
8 The supermarket doesn't (does not) sell English books.
9 Do dogs sleep at night?

⑩ Das present progressive

Exercise 1

1 (is doing) – is helping – are cutting
2 are tidying – is putting – is making
3 am watching
4 am having – am writing – is swimming – is trying – is barking – are sleeping

Exercise 2

2 Tweets is singing in her cage.
3 Kirsty is running to the bus stop.
4 Amy and Tom are practising a new dance.
5 Mrs Cobb is making a bed.
6 Adam is sleeping in bed.

Exercise 3

1 I am playing with my dog.
2 Tom is repairing his bike.
3 My parents are sleeping. Please be quiet!
4 I am tidying my room.
5 We are helping our parents in the kitchen.

Exercise 3

2 are not waiting at the station
3 is not cleaning
4 are not listening
5 am not making
6 are not putting away your

Exercise 4

2 Are you helping
3 Is Kirsty wearing
4 Are Miss Jones and Mr Carter sitting
5 Am I playing
6 Are we doing a German test
7 Is Adam eating sweets again

Super fast lane

am standing – am talking – am doing – Are you doing – am cutting – is listening – Are they practising – are making – is trying – is barking – are playing – Are you going

Super fast lane

1 is not running – is – runs – think – is not trying – are – is – wants
2 Are you tidying – are you playing – am tidying – play – put
3 are doing – are not working – thinks – hates – are choosing – like – are doing

Vokabelübungen 4

1 The magic tree

(three apples), two oranges, five strawberries, two bananas, four potatoes, four tomatoes, one (cabbage, and) six (carrots)

2 Find that animal

(The missing animal is the) zebra

⑪ Das going to-future

Exercise 1

2 is going to dance
3 is going to play
4 are going to work
5 are going to wash
6 is going to drive

Exercise 2

2 Mr Carter is not going to move.
3 Amy is not going to watch the football match next Saturday.
4 Amy and Tom aren't going to meet Mr Carter.
5 Mr and Mrs Parker aren't going to go to a concert.
6 Kirsty isn't going to see the new Walt Disney Film.

Exercise 3

2 Is Bob going to visit
3 Is Amy going to phone her friend Kirsty
4 Is Kirsty going to play tennis with Tom
5 Are we going to take the bus
6 Is Mrs Nunn going to have a shower after work

Vokabelübungen 5

1 Worträtsel

1 school
2 shops
3 supermarket
4 cinema
5 library
6 station
7 stadium

Lösungswort: chemist

2 Complete the sentences

1 B
2 A
3 C
4 A
5 B
6 B
7 B
8 C

4 because he always beats her.
5 when he finds his shoes.
6 because he eats so many sweets.
7 where her homework is.

Exercise 3

2 We are all going to the cinema in London on Saturday.
3 Mr Nunn goes to work at 7 o'clock every day.
4 The film is on at the youth club at 8.30 on Friday.
5 Adam is going to Athens in Greece this summer.
6 Miss Jones wants to move into her new flat in Penny Street at the weekend.

Exercise 4

2 Amy and Kirsty often go to the disco on Fridays.
3 Bob and Tom never meet at the youth club in Davis Street.
4 Mr Clarke usually helps Mrs Clarke with the housework.
5 Mrs Parker is always working in the garden.
6 Spooky is sometimes a naughty little dog.

⓬ Die Wortstellung

Exercise 1

2 Adam eats a lot of sweets.
3 Spooky is playing with Coco.
4 Mr Clarke is washing his new car.
5 Miss Jones is reading a book.
6 Mr and Mrs Parker are working in the garden.

Exercise 2

2 when the Cobbs are out.
3 because she makes the breakfast.

⓭ Fragewörter

Exercise 1

3 When does Kirsty get up every morning
4 Why do you like Miss Jones
5 Who are you going to see at the youth club disco
6 Where is the post office
7 How do I do the exercise
8 When is your birthday
9 How does Adam feel
10 Why is Bob wearing shorts

Exercise 2

3 What does Amy give Tweets every morning?
4 What are Adam's favourite sweets?
5 Which jacket does Bob like?
6 Which magic dictionary would you like to buy?

Exercise 3

2 Whose bird is Tweets?
3 Whose form teacher is Miss Jones?
4 Whose neighbour is Adam?
5 Whose bag is on the desk?

Exercise 4

2 Who
3 Who
4 What
5 Who
6 What

Super fast lane

2 Why is Bob happy?
3 What happens every day?
4 What are you doing?
5 Who is going out with Kirsty today?
6 Who does Amy love?
7 When do you have lunch?
8 Which blouse does Kirsty like?
9 Where does Kirsty Nunn live?
10 Whose computer game is it?

⓮ Mengenangaben

Exercise 1

2 some coffee – any tea
3 some cake – any biscuits
4 some postcards – any stamps
5 some books – any CDs
6 some dresses – any lipstick
7 some football boots – any footballs

Exercise 2

(bread) – butter – coffee – homework – lemonade – love – meat – milk – money – sugar – time – training – water

Exercise 3

1 a lot of
2 many/a lot of
3 much
4 much/a lot of – a lot of
5 many
6 A lot of/Many

Super fast lane

any – some – much – any – some – many – some – some/a lot of – some – some – any – any/much – much – some – a lot of – any/much – a lot of – any

⓯ Die Präpositionen

Exercise 1

2 behind
3 in/inside
4 outside
5 between
6 at
7 on
8 under
9 next to

Exercise 2

2 between
3 in front of
4 behind
5 between
6 in front of
7 next to
8 behind
9 between
10 next to

Exercise 3

(out of) – down – round – through – over – into – under – past – into

Exercise 4

1 at – in
2 in – at
3 on
4 in – at – at – at
5 in
6 on (at) – in
7 on – in

Super fast lane

1 at
2 on
3 in
4 on – at
5 in front of
6 at
7 towards
8 round
9 down
10 over – through
11 next to
12 in 2004 – in

Cornelsen online http://www.cornelsen.de

Dieses Werk berücksichtigt die Regeln der reformierten Rechtschreibung und Zeichensetzung.

5. 4. 3. 2. 1.
07 06 05 04 03 Die letzten Ziffern bezeichnen Zahl und Jahr der Auflage.

Printed in the Czech Republic
ISBN 3-589-21816-9
Bestellnummer 218169

Super fast lane

Übersetze die unterstrichenen Präpositionen ins Englische.

✔ = richtig ✘ = falsch

1 Der Unterricht fängt um 5 Uhr an. ________

2 In England ist Weihnachten am 25. Dezember. ________

3 Ostern ist meistens im April. ________

4 Der Test ist am Freitag um 9 Uhr. ________ ________

5 Ein Baum steht vor dem Haus. ________

6 Die Familie sitzt am Tisch. ________

7 Mr Carter kommt auf uns zu. ________

8 Spooky läuft um den Baum herum. ________

9 Bob läuft den Hügel hinunter. ________

10 Der Ball geht über den Zaun und durch das Fenster. ________ ________

11 Die Cobbs wohnen neben den Parkers. ________

12 Die nächste Weltausstellung ist 2004 in Japan. ________ ________

Weniger als 11 Punkte? Wenn ja, arbeite bitte Kapitel 15 A bis 15 C nochmals durch.

max. 15

Her mit den besseren Noten!

Das bewährte **Besser in …-Lernhilfenprogramm** gibt es komplett in Neuausgabe für Deutsch, Englisch und Mathematik von Klasse 5–10: Je ein vierfarbiger Band pro Fach und Jahrgang deckt alle wichtigen Lehrplanthemen ab.

Übungen, Tipps, Lösungshilfen und die wichtigsten Regeln zum Nachschlagen und Lernen für zu Hause und unterwegs. Mit separatem Lösungsheft – zur Selbstkontrolle oder für die Eltern.

	ISBN 3-589-
Deutsch 5. Klasse	21809-6
Deutsch 6. Klasse	21811-8
Deutsch 7. Klasse	21812-6
Deutsch 8. Klasse	21813-4
Deutsch 9. Klasse	21814-2
Deutsch 10. Klasse	21815-0

	ISBN 3-589-
Englisch 5. Klasse	21816-9
Englisch 6. Klasse	21817-7
Englisch 7. Klasse	21818-5
Englisch 8. Klasse	21819-3
Englisch 9. Klasse	21820-7
Englisch 10. Klasse	21821-5

	ISBN 3-589-
Mathe 5. Klasse	21822-3
Mathe 6. Klasse	21823-1
Mathe 7. Klasse	21825-8
Mathe 8. Klasse	21826-6
Mathe 9. Klasse	21827-4
Mathe 10. Klasse	21828-2

Die folgenden Titel liegen weiterhin in zweifarbiger Ausstattung vor:

	ISBN 3-589-
Französisch Grammatik 1. Lernjahr	21831-2
Französisch Grammatik 2. Lernjahr	21832-0
Französisch Grammatik 3./4. Lernjahr	21833-9
Latein Grammatik 1./2. Lernjahr	21830-4
Spanisch Grammatik 1./2. Lernjahr	21829-0

Cornelsen
Power Learning

Fragen Sie bitte in Ihrer Buchhandlung!